—YEAR-ROUND—
ROASTING

**RECIPES BY
MELANIE BARNARD, BRIGIT BINNS,
AMANDA HAAS, TORI RITCHIE,
RICK RODGERS, BOB & COLEEN SIMMONS,
AND THE EDITORS OF WILLIAMS-SONOMA**

PHOTOGRAPHS BY ERIC WOLFINGER

weldon**owen**

CONTENTS

ABOUT ROASTING

Roasting is one of the oldest and most traditional forms of cooking, yet it is still one of the most versatile and accessible ways to cook today. Whether it's a whole chicken, a holiday roast, or seasonal vegetables and fruits, the time these foods spend in the oven yields tender, juicy interiors and rich caramelized exteriors that no other technique can achieve. And because roasting is so simple—often all it takes is a bold seasoning and then waiting for the results—it is perfect for a busy lifestyle.

This book offers more than 100 recipes for a wide variety of foods. We've included recipes fit for a quick weekday meal or a relaxed Sunday supper, as well as recipes for holiday favorites such as roast turkey, standing rib roast, and leg of lamb, as well as seafood, vegetables, and fruits. Each chapter contains useful information on choosing, preparing, and cooking the main ingredient to perfection.

As you look through the recipes, you'll notice that roasting is an ideal way to cook almost any meal. The versatile method enhances natural flavors and can help create both indulgent as well as healthy meals, depending on your needs. These recipes will help set the stage for a memorable meal any time of the year and for any occasion.

BENEFITS OF ROASTING

Roasting refers to cooking food, uncovered, in the dry heat of an oven. There is something wonderfully elemental about this technique, a tradition with roots that reach back to when the first foods were cooked over an open fire. Today's oven-fired dishes retain a similar down-to-earth appeal: crusty and well browned on the outside, juicy and flavorful inside, and creating irresistible aromas that fill the whole house.

ROASTING IS VERSATILE

Roasting is best suited to tender cuts of meat, poultry, and seafood, and also works well with many fresh vegetables and fruits. It is possible to roast both small and large items, and each has its advantages. Large items, like a roast or whole bird, gain a caramelized crust or crisp skin while staying juicy and moist on the inside, for an appealing contrast. Small items, like poultry parts, fish, shellfish, and fresh fruits and vegetables, cook quickly, many gaining that prized crisp exterior from contact with the heat of the oven.

ROASTING IS PERFECT FOR ANY OCCASION

Roasting has long been a favored cooking method for the holidays, from the Thanksgiving turkey to the Christmas rib roast to the Passover leg of lamb. Conveniently, roasting is an ideal technique to draw upon during the general stress of the holiday season. The preparations are usually minimal: Light trimming, seasoning, stuffing, or marinating is typically all that is needed. Sometimes meats and poultry are tied with kitchen string to create a compact or uniform shape. But once the food is in the oven, your work is done, apart from the occasional basting or brushing of a glaze near the end of the cooking time. Consider, too, that many roasted items take less than an hour to cook, making it possible to put dinner on the table relatively quickly, even on the busiest of weekdays.

ROASTING ENHANCES FLAVOR

A well-browned crust is one of the most appealing qualities of roasted foods. Contact with the oven's dry heat causes sugars and proteins to form compounds on the surface similar to caramel, thus forming the deeply colored exterior. Meanwhile, the heat slowly penetrates to the center of the food, cooking it through while keeping it juicy and flavorful. But the browned crust of oven-roasted food is only part of the reason for its rich flavor: Roasting also cooks away surface moisture, concentrating the true character of foods and adding complexity. Roasting evaporates moisture from flavoring agents, too. For example, if a roast is basted with broth or wine, the liquid will reduce to a flavorful glaze that will make the resulting sauce more delicious.

ROASTING IS IDEAL FOR HEALTHY COOKING

It's true that roasting calls for added fat, but only enough to moisten the food lightly and encourage browning. Unlike many other cooking methods, roasting offers the healthful advantage of retaining many of the nutrients that are naturally present in the food.

THE ART OF ROASTING

The recipes in this book utilize three main types of roasting: traditional roasting, hybrid roasting, and pan roasting. The type of roasting that is employed depends on the type and size of the food that is being roasted.

TRADITIONAL ROASTING

Traditional roasting calls for cooking foods in the oven using steady heat. Depending on the item being roasted, this could be a high temperature (400°F/200°C or higher), a moderate temperature (350°–400°F/180°–200°C), or a low temperature (350°F/180°C and lower).

HIGH-TEMPERATURE ROASTING In general, high-temperature roasting practically guarantees a tasty, highly browned exterior, but overcooking, odors, spattering, and extra cleanup can be drawbacks. High-oven temperatures do not enhance tenderness, so choose tender, uniformly shaped cuts for best results.

MODERATE-TEMPERATURE ROASTING Roasting using moderate temperatures minimizes shrinkage and moisture loss, leaving more natural moisture in the food. This type of roasting needs little monitoring, leaving you free to turn your attention to other tasks. Depending on the food and the relative temperature, foods roasted with moderate heat may not brown deeply. The best candidates for this technique are relatively tender meats, poultry, and fish with a high ratio good amount of fat.

LOW-TEMPERATURE ROASTING Also known as slow-roasting, this technique causes liquids to evaporate slowly, keeping foods juicy and keeping shrinkage and weight loss to a minimum. Cooking times are typically long, which helps melt large pockets of fat and break down connective tissues in tough cuts of meat. Slow-roasting can sometimes last for 3 hours or more, but its results promise falling-off-the-bone tenderness.

HYBRID ROASTING

Hybrid roasting utilizes more than one temperature range to offer benefits from each. For example, some recipes start with a high oven temperature to start the browning process, and then call for reducing the oven heat to finish the cooking process and minimize shrinkage and cleanup. Other recipes do the reverse: The food is started at a moderate temperature, reducing shrinkage and promoting juiciness, then is finished at a high temperature to encourage a well-browned crust.

ROASTING SAFETY

When working with raw meats and poultry, it is important to be especially vigilant to avoid food-borne illness. Use clean tools and cutting boards for food preparation and wash them thoroughly with hot soapy water after using them to cut raw meat or poultry. Thoroughly wash your hands with soap and hot running water before and after handling raw foods. Do not let cutting boards or knives used to prepare raw meats or poultry come in contact with the cooked meat or poultry, or with any foods you do not plan to cook, such as vegetables, fruits, fresh herbs, etc. Take extra care, too, with leftover marinades or glazes that may have come in contact with raw meat or poultry. When basting, stop using the marinade or glaze at least 10 minutes before the food is done, or be sure to boil the marinade or glaze for at least 2 minutes before basting the food again with it, or passing the marinade or glaze as a table sauce.

PAN ROASTING

This technique is borrowed from restaurant chefs, who need to ensure that every order is cooked quickly and consistently time after time. This two-level technique adds caramelized flavor to thin cuts of meat, poultry pieces, and seafood, and it supplies plenty of pan drippings for sauce. In pan-roasting, meat, poultry, or seafood is first seared on the stove top in a frying pan over high heat to brown the outer surface. Next, the pan is placed in a preheated oven, where the food roasts until it has finished cooking. While the roasted food rests on a plate or carving board, the pan drippings are often dissolved in wine or stock and quickly transformed into a sauce. A heavy, ovenproof frying pan is a must for pan-roasting. Flimsy pans or pans with plastic handles will not stand up to the high heat of the stove top or the oven.

ADDING FLAVOR TO ROASTED FOODS

There are many ways to add flavor before roasting foods, including rolling and tying meats with a bold filling, stuffing a savory mixture into a turkey cavity, rubbing flavored butter under the skin of a plump chicken, applying a bold glaze before roasting a tenderloin, or pressing a tasty bread-crumb mixture on the exterior of meats or fish. In addition to these methods, there are three common ways to enhance roasted foods: dry rubs, marinades, and brines.

DRY RUBS Dry rubs are mixtures of spices, herbs, and salt, often in the form of powders and pastes, which are pressed into the surface of meats or poultry. They work by drawing the food's juices to the surface and infusing them with flavor before they're naturally absorbed back into the food. A dry rub that contains a large percentage of salt by volume is sometimes referred to as a dry brine, and acts similarly to a brine (see below) without requiring a large volume of liquid.

MARINADES Marinades, a highly flavored mixture of liquids, spices, and herbs, add moisture to foods and can have a tenderizing effect when they include an acidic liquid. Marinades typically require some time to work, so read the recipe thoroughly in the event you need to plan ahead.

BRINES Brines, salt-based solutions used to soak meat or poultry, enhance the food's juiciness and distribute flavor throughout the flesh. Brines call for kosher salt, which is free of additives, but other flavorings can be added, like spices, sugar, and vinegar or another acidic ingredient. As the food soaks, the salt penetrates deep inside, drawing in moisture and other seasonings.

CHOOSING A ROASTING VESSEL

Whether you are using a roasting pan, baking sheet, frying pan, or other ovenproof container, choose one that holds the ingredients comfortably, leaving room for the oven's heat to circulate without trapping moisture. This will help ensure you get the prized browned crust that is the hallmark of expertly roasted foods.

LET IT REST

Roasted meats—and poultry, to a lesser degree—benefit from a resting time of 5–30 minutes before serving. This time allows the temperature of the meat to even out and the juices to disperse throughout the meat.

MEAT

BEEF

FILETS MIGNONS WITH TRUFFLE BUTTER 25

PAN-ROASTED PORTERHOUSE STEAK 26

STEAK AU POIVRE 28

ROASTED FLANK STEAK STUFFED WITH OLIVES & PECORINO 29

BEEF TENDERLOIN WITH MADEIRA SAUCE 31

ARGENTINIAN-STYLE STUFFED FLANK STEAK 33

STANDING RIB ROAST WITH MADEIRA JUS & YORKSHIRE PUDDING 36

RIB-EYE ROAST WITH MUSTARD & BREAD CRUMB CRUST 39

STRIP LOIN ROAST WITH BRANDY SAUCE 40

NEW YORK STRIP STEAKS WITH HORSERADISH CREAM 41

LAMB

PAN-ROASTED T-BONE LAMB CHOPS WITH SALSA VERDE 43

RACK OF LAMB WITH SPICY CRANBERRY RELISH 44

BABY LAMB CHOPS WITH FIG-BALSAMIC PAN SAUCE 46

HERB-CRUSTED LAMB CHOPS 47

SLOW-ROASTED LAMB SHANKS WITH OLIVES & PRESERVED LEMON 49

LEG OF LAMB WITH SAUTÉED RADICCHIO 50

LEG OF LAMB STUFFED WITH PEPPERS & ONIONS 52

LAMB SHOULDER WITH SAUSAGE, LEEK & ONION STUFFING 53

LEG OF LAMB STUFFED WITH LEMON-OLIVE TAPENADE 55

LEG OF LAMB WITH BREAD CRUMB CRUST 56

PORK

FENNEL-CRUSTED PORK TENDERLOIN 57

CUBAN-STYLE PORK WITH MOJO DE AJO 58

PORK WITH APPLE-GINGER COMPOTE 60

PORK WITH SWEET & SOUR ONIONS 61

HERB-STUFFED PORK LOIN 62

CARIBBEAN-STYLE BRINED PORK CHOPS 63

APRICOT-STUFFED PORK LOIN 65

HERB-RUBBED PORK LOIN WITH RATATOUILLE 66

TUSCAN-STYLE PORK ROAST WITH FENNEL 67

BONE-IN PORK LOIN WITH MEDITERRANEAN FLAVORS 68

FIVE-SPICE PORK SHOULDER WITH GREEN ONION SALSA 71

BARBECUE-STYLE BABY BACK RIBS 72

MEAT FOR ROASTING

Roasting is ideal for tender cuts of meat that come from the less exercised parts of the animal. In general, meat toward the center of the animal and furthest away from the extremities tends to be the most tender. But many less tender cuts can be successfully roasted using a low temperature and a long cooking time. Both bone-in and boneless meats, in both small and large cuts, are good candidates for roasting. Good marbling—streaks of fat that run through the meat—translates to good flavor and moisture in the meat as it roasts. Some lean meats, such as pork loin or pork chops, benefit from being soaked in a brine to add flavor and moisture during the roasting process.

All meat sold in the U.S. is graded for wholesomeness. Grading for quality, however, is voluntary on the part of the producer. While a higher grade of meat means rich flavor and good texture after cooking, tenderness is usually a function of the cut. For example, beef brisket will have a chewy texture that requires long cooking, irrespective of its grade. Beef tenderloin, on the other hand, will almost always be tender, no matter how it is graded. For the best results, seek out a quality local butcher who has high turnover, and make them your resource for any questions you have about meats and how to cook them. If you purchase quality meat to begin with, all you will need are simple seasonings to bring out the meat's natural flavors.

BEEF

CHOOSING The best cuts for roasting include flank steak (stuffed and rolled), tenderloin, rib roast, strip loin roast, thick filets mignons, and thick bone-in steaks, such as Porterhouse. Nowadays, good-quality beef is available from many sources. Grass-fed beef, which is touted as being a healthy and environmentally sound choice, is becoming more and more popular.

PREPPING Remove any sinew and excess pockets of fat. Trim fat to about ¼ inch (6 mm) if necessary. Bring to room temperature before cooking.

STORING Keep beef up to 3 days in the refrigerator, or 6 months in the freezer before cooking.

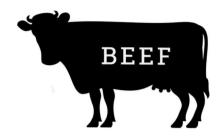

RARE 125°F (52°C)
MEDIUM-RARE 130°F (54°C)
MEDIUM 135°F (57°C)
MEDIUM-WELL 140°F (60°C)
WELL 150°F (65°C)

LAMB

CHOOSING The best cuts for roasting include the rack, shanks, leg (bone-in and boneless), shoulder, and thick chops. More than any other meat you can buy, lamb can vary in its characteristics due to the diversity of the breeds, their diets, and the climates in which the animals were raised. Ask your butcher for information about the flavor profile of the lamb sold in their shop.

PREPPING Trim the fat thoroughly to prevent the finished dish from having an overly gamy flavor. Bring to room temperature before cooking.

STORING Keep up to 2 days in the refrigerator, or 6 months in the freezer.

RARE 125°F (52°C)
MEDIUM-RARE 130°F (54°C)
MEDIUM 135°F (57°C)
MEDIUM-WELL 140°F (60°C)
WELL 150°F (65°C)

PORK

CHOOSING The best cuts for roasting include the loin (bone-in or boneless), tenderloin, shoulder, ribs, and thick chops. In the U.S., pork is not as intensively graded as beef. In the absence of grades, knowing how to identify high-quality meat is very important. For the best flavor and most humane treatment of the animals, seek out pork from heritage breeds from a quality butcher.

PREPPING Resist the urge to trim away too much fat from good pork. Fat carries flavor and keeps the meat moist. Remove the silver skin from pork tenderloin. Bring to room temperature before cooking.

STORING Keep up to 2 days in the refrigerator, or 6 months in the freezer.

MEDIUM 135°F (57°C)
MEDIUM-WELL 140°F (60°C)
WELL 150°F (65°C)

HOW TO ROAST MEAT

1 PREP

Prep the meat for cooking. Trim it as directed and bring it to room temperature (about 30 minutes for small cuts or up to 2 hours for large roasts). Preheat the oven thoroughly.

2 FLAVOR

Flavor the meat with simple seasonings, a marinade, or brine. If a long soak is needed, you'll want to bring the meat to room temperature and preheat the oven (see Step 1) afterwards.

3 BROWN

Brown the meat, if called for, aiming for a deep burnished look on all sides of the meat. Use a large set of tongs to turn the meat to brown all sides.

4 ROAST

Put the meat in the oven and let it roast, paying attention to the cues in the recipe for turning or basting the meat as needed.

5 CHECK

Test the meat for doneness using an instant-read thermometer. For an accurate reading, insert the thermometer into the center of the meat, not touching any bones or fatty areas.

6 REST

Be sure to let the meat rest for 5–20 minutes, depending on the size. During this time, the meat will continue to cook a bit, while the juices are being reabsorbed throughout.

7 FINISH

Depending on how they are flavored, some meats can be served right after they rest, but for others you might want to make a sauce from the pan drippings. Follow the cues in the recipe.

CARVING A BONELESS ROAST

Carving a roast into uniform pieces helps make a beautiful presentation. Evenly sliced pieces can be layered on a plate or platter for serving.

1 ARRANGE ON A BOARD

Set the roast on a large cutting board, ideally one with grooves to collect any juices that may seep from the meat during carving.

2 STEADY WITH A FORK

Use a large carving fork to hold the roast in place on the board. Try to avoid inserting the tines into the meat.

3 CUT INTO SLICES

Position a large knife opposite the direction of the muscle fibers so that it will cut the meat across the grain. Cut it into slices ¼–½ inch (6–12 mm) thick.

CARVING A BONE-IN ROAST

Carving a bone-in roast may seem intimidating, but if you break it down into distinct steps, the process is simple.

1 ARRANGE ON A BOARD

Place the meat bone side down on a large cutting board, ideally one with grooves to collect any juices that may seep from the meat during carving.

2 STEADY WITH A FORK

Use a large carving fork to hold the roast in place on the board. Try to avoid inserting the tines into the meat.

3 CUT INTO SLICES

Using a long knife, cut the meat between the bones into large, thick slices.

BUTTERFLYING BONELESS MEAT CUTS

Butterflying large pieces of meat, like a leg of lamb or pork loin, creates a thin, flat piece that can be stuffed, rolled, and tied.

1 CUT THE MEAT LENGTHWISE

Make a cut down the length of the meat, following the muscle of the meat and cutting from one side to the other without cutting all the way through.

2 LAY THE MEAT FLAT

Open the meat as if opening a book so that the piece of meat is roughly flat. It should resemble a large, lumpy rectangle.

3 EVEN IT OUT

Cut an inch (2.5 cm) or so into the thickest parts of the meat, then open them out like the pages of a book, flattening the flaps in the opposite direction. The rectangle should be about 1 inch (2.5 cm) thick.

Velvety-textured thick-cut filets mignons are always impressive for a dinner party. Here's a special recipe that is actually very simple to pull off. Truffle salt is a great ingredient to have on hand to lend additional depth to your dishes. It's great with steak, potato, and pasta dishes. Look for it in well-stocked grocery stores or at specialty purveyors.

FILETS MIGNONS WITH TRUFFLE BUTTER

6 tablespoons (3 oz/90 g) unsalted butter, at room temperature

¾ teaspoon truffle salt

6 filets mignons, each about 6 oz (185 g)

Kosher salt and freshly ground pepper

Canola oil, for coating

Snipped fresh chives, for garnish (optional)

SERVES 6

The day before you plan to roast, place the butter in a medium bowl and sprinkle it with the truffle salt. Using a fork, mash the salt into the butter. Scrape the butter onto a sheet of plastic wrap. Lift the plastic wrap over the butter and gently shape the butter into a log. Fold the ends of plastic wrap around the log and refrigerate overnight.

Remove the filets mignons from the refrigerator about 30 minutes before roasting. Preheat the oven to 450°F (230°C).

Heat a large, heavy ovenproof frying pan over high heat until it is very hot, about 3 minutes. Generously season the filets mignons all over with salt and pepper. Add just enough oil to coat the bottom of the pan. When the oil is shimmering, add the steaks and sear for about 5 minutes. Turn the steaks and transfer the pan to the oven. Roast until an instant-read thermometer inserted into the thickest part of the meat registers 130°F (54°C) for medium-rare, 3–4 minutes, or until done to your liking.

Meanwhile, cut the truffle butter into 6 equal slices. Arrange the filets mignons on warmed individual plates and top each with a pat of butter. Garnish with the chives, if using. Serve right away.

Dinner for two? Try this recipe for a premium steak that utilizes an initial high-heat searing process followed by a long resting period, and then a final stint in the oven. The process helps the juices to remain in the meat while the heat migrates slowly toward the center. Serve with creamy white beans and Asparagus with Shallots & Lemon (page 170).

PAN-ROASTED PORTERHOUSE STEAK

1 porterhouse steak, about 1½ lb (750 g), patted dry

1 tablespoon olive oil, plus oil as needed

Kosher salt and freshly ground pepper

SERVES 2 OR 3

Rub the steak all over with 1 tablespoon oil. Let stand at room temperature for 1–1½ hours.

Heat a large ovenproof frying pan over high heat until it is very hot, about 3 minutes. Generously season the steak all over with salt and pepper. Add just enough oil to the pan to coat the bottom and reduce the heat to medium-high. When the oil is shimmering, use tongs to place the steak in the pan, and sear for 2½ minutes on each side. Transfer to a rack set over a plate and let stand at room temperature for 30 minutes or up to 1 hour.

Preheat the oven to 425°F (220°C).

Return the steak to the pan, transfer to the oven, and roast until an instant-read thermometer inserted into the thickest part of the steak away from the bone registers 130°F (54°C) for medium-rare, about 12 minutes, or until done to your liking. Transfer to the rack and let rest, uncovered, for 5–8 minutes.

Transfer to a carving board and cut the sirloin away from the bone on one side and the filet section on the other. Cut against the grain into thick slices. Arrange on warmed individual plates. Serve right away, passing oil at the table for drizzling.

This classic dish is reminiscent of old-school steakhouse fare. The tender filet mignon steaks are prepared with a two-step roasting method, which ensures they are juicy in the center and crusty on the outside. An easy green peppercorn–laced pan sauce comes together quickly.

STEAK AU POIVRE

4 filets mignons, each about 7 oz (220 g), patted dry

1½ tablespoons olive oil, plus oil as needed

¼ cup (2 oz/60 g) dried or brine-packed green peppercorns, drained if necessary

Kosher salt and coarsely cracked pepper

1 tablespoon unsalted butter

1 large shallot, minced

3 tablespoons brandy or Cognac

½ cup (4 fl oz/125 ml) heavy cream

¼ cup (2 fl oz/60 ml) prepared beef consommé

SERVES 4

Rub the steaks all over with the oil. Let stand at room temperature for 1 hour.

In a small saucepan, combine the peppercorns with cold water to cover. Bring to a boil and boil for 1 minute. Drain and set aside.

Preheat the oven to 425°F (220°C). Heat a large, ovenproof frying pan over high heat until it is very hot, about 3 minutes. Generously season the steaks all over with salt and pepper. Add just enough oil to the pan to coat the bottom, and reduce the heat to medium-high. When the oil is shimmering, use tongs to place the steaks in the pan, without letting them touch. Sear for 2 minutes on each side. Transfer to a rack set over a plate and let stand for 30 minutes.

Return the steaks to the pan; transfer to the oven, and roast until an instant-read thermometer inserted into the thickest part of a steak registers 130°F (54°C) for medium-rare, about 9 minutes, or until done to your liking. Transfer the steaks to the rack and let rest, uncovered, while you prepare the sauce.

In the same frying pan, melt the butter over medium heat. Add the shallot and cook, stirring, until softened, about 2 minutes. Add the peppercorns and stir for 1 minute. Add the brandy and ignite it with a long-handled match. Cook, shaking the pan gently, until the flames die down. Stir in the cream and consommé, raise the heat to medium-high, and simmer until thickened, about 2 minutes.

Return the steaks to the pan, spoon the sauce over the top, and heat until the steaks are warmed through, about 1 minute. Taste the sauce and adjust the seasonings. Serve right away.

Flank steak, stuffed with a vibrant filling, rolled, and tied before roasting is a crowd-pleasing main course. This version is filled with a collection of Italian-inspired ingredients: meaty prosciutto, bright-green herbs, salty sheep's-milk cheese, and briny green olives.

To butterfly the flank steak, place the steak at the edge of a cutting board with a short side toward you and the edge of the narrower long side on your right (reverse if you are left-handed). Using a long, thin-bladed knife, cut the meat almost in half through the narrower side, from right to left (or vice versa). Open it as you would a book. Using a mallet, pound the steak lightly to flatten it to an even thickness. Ideally, you want a rough square of meat that is 12–15 inches (30–38 cm).

Preheat the oven to 350°F (180°C).

Lightly season the cut side of the meat with salt and pepper. Lay the prosciutto slices in an even layer running across the grain from top to bottom. In a medium bowl, stir together the cheese, olives, bread crumbs, garlic, oregano, sage, vinegar, and 2 tablespoons of the oil. Spread the mixture evenly over the prosciutto, leaving 3 inches (7.5 cm) of one side of the meat uncovered. Roll up the meat around the filling, working toward the uncovered side, to form a roll. Using kitchen string, tie the roll crosswise at regular intervals, forming a compact cylinder.

In a roasting pan just large enough to hold the rolled meat, warm the remaining 1 tablespoon oil on the stove top over medium-high heat. When it is very hot, sear the meat until browned on all sides, 12–15 minutes. Transfer to the oven and roast until an instant-read thermometer inserted into the thickest part of the roll registers 130°F (54°C) for medium-rare, 25–30 minutes, or until done to your liking. Transfer to a carving board and tent with aluminum foil. Let rest for 15–30 minutes.

Snip the strings and cut into thick slices. Serve right away.

ROASTED FLANK STEAK STUFFED WITH OLIVES & PECORINO

1 flank steak, 1½–1¾ lb (750–875 g)

Kosher salt and freshly ground pepper

5 very thin slices prosciutto

6 oz (185 g) pecorino romano, grated

1 can (about 5 oz/165 g) anchovy-stuffed green olives, drained and finely chopped, or 1¼ cups (6 oz/185 g) brine-cured green olives, pitted and coarsely chopped

¾ cup (1½ oz/45 g) seasoned dried bread crumbs, toasted until golden

6 cloves garlic, minced

3 tablespoons coarsely chopped fresh oregano

1 tablespoon minced fresh sage

1 tablespoon red wine vinegar

3 tablespoons extra-virgin olive oil

SERVES 6

A whole beef tenderloin is the ideal roast for a celebratory meal. The roast is done in a relatively short time, so the sweet onions are first cooked on top of the stove, then cooled slightly before being used as a flavorful roasting rack. If you can't find the Madeira, you can substitute tawny Port. Accompany the tenderloin with Fingerling Potatoes with Garlic & Thyme (page 183).

Using a sharp, thin-bladed knife, remove the chain muscle, the long, thin side muscle with connective tissue and fat that runs almost the entire length of the tenderloin. Reserve for another use, such as stir-frying or making ground beef, or discard. Then, remove the silver skin and most of the surface fat from the tenderloin. Next, fold over the narrow end piece toward the thicker portion to make a uniformly thick cylinder. Using kitchen string, tie the roll crosswise at regular intervals, forming a compact cylinder. Place the tenderloin on a platter. Rub the meat on all sides with 2 tablespoons of the olive oil and season generously with salt and pepper, rubbing the seasonings in with your fingertips. (At this point, the roast can be refrigerated uncovered for up to 24 hours. Remove it from the refrigerator about 1 hour before roasting.)

In a large frying pan over low heat, warm the remaining 2 tablespoons oil. Add the onions, stir to coat with the oil, and season with salt and pepper. Cook for 2–3 minutes, then add ¼ cup (2 fl oz/60 ml) water, the thyme sprigs, and balsamic vinegar. Cover and cook over low heat, stirring occasionally, until the onions are very soft but not browned, about 15 minutes. Uncover. If any liquid remains in the bottom of the pan, raise the heat to medium-high and cook, stirring, just until the liquid evaporates. Do not let the onions color.

Position a rack in the upper third of the oven and preheat to 425°F (220°C). Arrange the onions down the center of a shallow roasting pan just large enough to hold the tenderloin (or on the diagonal if you have a larger roast) to form a natural roasting rack. Place the tenderloin on the onions. *continued*

BEEF TENDERLOIN WITH MADEIRA SAUCE

1 whole beef tenderloin, about 4 lb (2 kg)

¼ cup (2 fl oz/60 ml) olive oil

Kosher salt and freshly ground pepper

5 large sweet onions, 2½ lb (2.25 kg) total weight, thinly sliced

2 fresh thyme sprigs

1 tablespoon balsamic vinegar

continued

SERVES 10–12

FOR THE SAUCE

½ cup (4 fl oz/125 ml)
Bual Madeira, plus
more as needed

3 cups (24 fl oz/750 ml) beef
stock or low-sodium broth

2–3 tablespoons
beef demi-glace

1 tablespoon red wine
vinegar

Kosher salt and freshly
ground pepper

2 tablespoons unsalted
butter, at room temperature

2 tablespoons
all-purpose flour

Roast the tenderloin until an instant-read thermometer inserted into the thickest part of the meat registers 130°F (54°C) for medium-rare, about 45 minutes, or until done to your liking.

Remove the roasting pan from the oven, transfer the tenderloin to a platter, and tent with aluminum foil. Let the meat rest for 10–15 minutes.

Meanwhile, to make the sauce, in a saucepan over medium-high heat, bring the Madeira to a boil and cook until reduced to ¼ cup (2 fl oz/60 ml). Pour about ½ cup (4 fl oz/125 ml) of the pan juices from the roasting pan into the saucepan through a fine-mesh sieve. Discard the thyme and reserve the onions in the pan until serving. Add the beef stock to the saucepan, bring to a boil, and cook for 2–3 minutes to reduce slightly and blend the flavors. Reduce the heat to medium-low and stir in the demi-glace and red wine vinegar. Season to taste with salt and pepper and 2–3 tablespoons more Madeira, if desired.

Using a fork, mix together the butter and flour in a small bowl. Reduce the heat under the sauce to low, whisk the butter mixture into the liquid a little at a time, and simmer until the sauce thickens slightly, 2–3 minutes. Keep the sauce warm.

Transfer the tenderloin to a carving board. To serve, snip the strings and cut the roast crosswise into thick slices. Place a spoonful of the sweet onions on each warmed individual plate and top with 2 tenderloin slices. Spoon a little of the sauce over the meat and serve right away. Pass the remaining sauce at the table.

This flank steak, stuffed with a savory vegetable and meat stuffing, is just the ticket to satisfy a hearty meat craving.

ARGENTINIAN-STYLE STUFFED FLANK STEAK

Lay the steak flat on a cutting board. Season the steak with salt and pepper and sprinkle with the vinegar, garlic, and thyme leaves. Let stand at room temperature for 30 minutes.

To make the stuffing, bring a saucepan of lightly salted water to a boil. Add the carrots and simmer until tender, about 10 minutes. Drain and transfer to paper towels. In a frying pan, pour water to a depth of ½ inch (12 mm). Bring to a simmer, then add the sausages. Cover the pan and cook the sausages for 10 minutes. Transfer the sausages to paper towels to drain. Halve the sausages lengthwise.

Preheat the oven to 375°F (190°C). Position the steak with the long edge facing you. Starting 1 inch (2.5 cm) in from the edge closest to you, cover the steak with half of the spinach, stopping about 3 inches (7.5 cm) short of the opposite edge. Distribute half of the cheese over the spinach leaves. Starting about 1½ inches (4 cm) in from the edge closest to you, arrange a row of carrots parallel to the grain of the meat. Leave about a ½-inch (12-mm) gap and then arrange a row of pepper strips. Leave another ½-inch gap, and arrange 2 sausage halves. Repeat the rows of carrots, pepper, and sausage until the spinach is covered. Distribute the remaining cheese evenly over the rows, and then cover with the remaining spinach. Starting at the edge nearest to you, fold over the flap of steak and roll the meat around the filling to form a compact cylinder. Using kitchen string, secure the cylinder at regular intervals. Season the roll with salt and pepper.

In a heavy ovenproof frying pan just large enough to hold the meat, warm the oil on the stove top over high heat. Add the meat and sear on all sides. Transfer to the oven and roast until an instant-read thermometer inserted into the thickest part of the meat roll registers 130°F (54°C) for medium-rare, about 40 minutes, or until done to your liking. Transfer to a carving board and tent with aluminum foil. Let rest for 15–20 minutes.

Snip the strings and cut the roll into slices. Serve warm.

1 large flank steak, 1½–2 lb (750 g–1 kg), butterflied (page 23), and pounded lightly to an even thickness

Kosher salt and freshly ground pepper

1 tablespoon red wine vinegar

2 cloves garlic, minced

1 teaspoon fresh thyme leaves

1 tablespoon olive oil

FOR THE STUFFING

Kosher salt and freshly ground pepper

2 large carrots, peeled and halved lengthwise

2 sweet Italian sausages

24 large spinach leaves

2 cups (8 oz/250 g) coarsely shredded provolone cheese

1 large red bell pepper, roasted, peeled, and seeded, then sliced into strips

SERVES 8

Seasoned with mustard, rosemary, and thyme and served with a Madeira jus, this standing rib roast is rich in flavor and classic in presentation (it's a traditional Christmas dish in Britain). If you are serving this for a special-occasion meal, ask the butcher to remove the roast's chine bone to ease carving, and to shorten and French the ribs for a nice presentation.

STANDING RIB ROAST WITH MADEIRA JUS & YORKSHIRE PUDDING

2 tablespoons Dijon mustard

1 tablespoon olive oil

1 tablespoon chopped fresh thyme

1 tablespoon chopped fresh rosemary

2 cloves garlic, chopped

Kosher salt and freshly ground pepper

1 standing rib roast, about 6–6½ lb (3–3.25 kg), frenched with 3 or 4 ribs

FOR THE MADEIRA JUS

2 cups (16 fl oz/500 ml) dry Madeira

2 tablespoons beef or veal demi-glace

continued

SERVES 6

In a small bowl, stir together the mustard, olive oil, thyme, rosemary, and garlic with 1 tablespoon salt and 2 teaspoons pepper to form a paste. Rub the paste all over the entire roast and let stand at room temperature for 1 hour.

Position a rack in the lower third of the oven and preheat the oven to 450°F (230°C).

Place the roast, bone side down, in a roasting pan and roast for 15 minutes. Reduce the oven temperature to 350°F (180°C) and continue to roast until an instant-read thermometer inserted into the thickest part of the roast away from the bone registers 130°F (54°C) for medium-rare, about 1 hour and 40 minutes longer, or until done to your liking. Transfer the roast to a warmed serving platter and tent with aluminum foil. Let rest for 15–20 minutes.

Meanwhile, make the Madeira jus: Use a large spoon to skim off the fat from the drippings in the roasting pan, and reserve the fat for making the Yorkshire pudding (see page 38). Place the roasting pan over medium-high heat and stir the Madeira into the pan juices, scraping up the brown bits from the bottom of the pan. Whisk in the demi-glace and any meat juices from the serving platter. Continue to cook, stirring occasionally, until the liquid is reduced by half, 8–10 minutes longer. Pour the jus through a fine-mesh sieve into a warmed serving bowl and skim off any fat that rises to the surface. *continued*

FOR THE YORKSHIRE PUDDING

1 cup (5 oz/155 g) all-purpose flour

1 tablespoon chopped fresh thyme

½ teaspoon dry mustard

Kosher salt and freshly ground pepper

3 large eggs

1 cup (8 fl oz/250 ml) half-and-half

6 teaspoons rendered beef fat from the roasting pan

To make the Yorkshire pudding, in a large bowl, whisk together the flour, thyme, mustard, ½ teaspoon each salt and pepper, eggs, and half-and-half to form a smooth batter.

Once the roast is removed from the oven, carefully position the rack in the middle, and then raise the temperature to 450°F (230°C). Place an empty 12-cup muffin pan in the oven to heat for 5 minutes. Remove the pan from the oven and brush ½ teaspoon of the rendered beef fat on the bottom and sides of each muffin cup. Stir the batter lightly if any separation has occurred. Divide the batter evenly among the 12 muffin cups. Bake the puddings until golden and crisp, about 15 minutes.

Remove the puddings from the oven and, using a table knife, loosen the sides of each pudding to remove them from the pan. Transfer to a basket and wrap in a cloth napkin to keep warm.

Carve the roast tableside, offering the end slices to those who prefer their meat cooked medium and the center slices to those who prefer it more rare, and arrange on warmed individual plates. Serve right away, passing the warm Yorkshire puddings and the jus at the table.

Beef rib roast is a decadent cut with generous marbling. The rich veins of fat melt during roasting and baste the meat from the inside out, creating juicy results. Mustard and bread crumbs add a satisfying crunch to the golden exterior.

RIB-EYE ROA
WITH MUSTA
& BREAD CRU
CRUST

Using a sharp knife, trim the surface fat from the roast to about ¼ inch (6 mm). Let stand at room temperature for 1½ hours.

Preheat the oven to 500°F (260°C).

Cut slits about ½ inch (12 mm) deep all over the roast, spacing them about 2 inches (5 cm) apart. Insert a sliver of anchovy and garlic into each slit. Place the roast, fat side up, on a rack in a roasting pan. Brush the top lightly with oil and season all sides generously with salt. Roast until the fat is sizzling and golden, about 20 minutes.

Meanwhile, prepare the crust: In a bowl, whisk together the mustard, oil, and thyme. Stir in the bread crumbs and season to taste with pepper.

Remove the roast from the oven and press the crust mixture over the top of the beef, compressing it into a firm layer. Reduce the oven temperature to 325°F (165°C). Roast until an instant-read thermometer inserted into the thickest part of the roast registers 130° (54°) for medium-rare, 1¼–1½ hours, or until done to your liking. Transfer the roast to a platter and tent with aluminum foil. Let rest for 8–10 minutes. Carve into thin slices. Serve at once, accompanied by the lemon wedges.

1 boneless rib-eye roast, 3½–4 lb (1.75–2 kg)

6 anchovy fillets, packed in salt, soaked in water fo 10 minutes, then drained, patted dry, and chopped

4 cloves garlic, thinly slic

Olive oil, for brushing

Kosher salt

FOR THE CRUST

⅓ cup (3 oz/90 g) whole-grain mustard

3 tablespoons olive oil

1 tablespoon dried thyme

1 cup (2 oz/60 g) fresh bread crumbs

Freshly ground pepper

Lemon wedges, for servir

SERVES 6–8

STRIP LOIN ROAST WITH BRANDY SAUCE

1 boneless beef strip loin
roast, about 3 lb (1.5 kg)

Kosher salt

1 teaspoon freshly ground
pepper

1 teaspoon chopped
fresh thyme

⅓ cup (3 fl oz/80 ml) brandy

¾ cup (6 fl oz/180 ml)
heavy cream

½ cup (4 fl oz/125 ml)
beef or chicken stock
or low-sodium broth

SERVES 6

Strip loin roast is the cut of beef from which New York strip steaks are cut. A good butcher will cut the roast to order and trim any excess fat. Mashed potatoes are the perfect accompaniment for soaking up the brandy-spiked sauce.

Using a sharp knife, trim the surface fat from the roast to ⅛ inch (3 mm). Season the roast all over with salt. Turn the roast fat side up and rub the pepper and thyme on the fat. Let stand at room temperature for 1 hour.

Preheat the oven to 450°F (230°C).

Oil a flat roasting rack and place it in a flameproof roasting pan just large enough to hold the roast. Place the meat fat side up on the rack. Roast for 15 minutes. Reduce the oven temperature to 375°F (190°C) and continue to roast until an instant-read thermometer inserted into the thickest part of the meat registers 130°F (54°C) for medium-rare, about 45 minutes, or until done to your liking.

Transfer the meat to a warmed platter and tent with aluminum foil. Let rest for 10–15 minutes.

Meanwhile, remove the rack from the pan and use a large spoon to skim off the fat from the drippings. Pour the brandy into the pan. Place the pan on the stove top over medium-high heat and bring the liquid to a strong simmer. Simmer briefly, stirring to scrape up the browned bits on the pan bottom. Pour the contents of the roasting pan into a small saucepan and add the cream and stock. Bring to a boil over medium-high heat and cook, stirring occasionally, until the sauce is slightly thickened and reduced by half, about 10 minutes. Season to taste with salt.

Transfer the roast to a carving board and pour any juices from the platter into the brandy sauce. Cut the meat across the grain into thick slices. Arrange the slices on warmed individual plates and spoon the sauce over the slices. Serve right away.

Boneless New York strip steaks, a restaurant-menu favorite, are easily pan-roasted at home for a special dinner. A zesty sauce of horseradish, mustard, and cream accompanies the meat. Serve with creamed spinach or roasted asparagus.

NEW YORK STRIP STEAKS WITH HORSERADISH CREAM

Using a sharp knife, trim away most of the fat from the steaks. Brush or rub the steaks on both sides with olive oil and season them with salt and pepper. Allow the steaks to stand at room temperature for about 30 minutes before roasting.

Preheat the oven to 450°F (230°C).

To make the cream, in a small bowl, whisk the heavy cream until soft peaks form. Fold in the horseradish, mustard, ¼ teaspoon salt, and the hot-pepper sauce. Spoon the sauce into a serving bowl and refrigerate until serving.

Preheat a large, heavy frying pan over high heat until very hot. Add the steaks and sear for 2 minutes on the first side. Turn the steaks and sear for 1 minute on the second side. Immediately place the pan in the oven and roast the steaks until a thermometer inserted into the center of the meat registers 125°F–130°F (52°C–54°C) for medium-rare, 6–7 minutes. Remove the pans from the oven, transfer the steaks to a warmed platter, and tent with aluminum foil. Let rest for 3–4 minutes.

Transfer the steaks to a carving board. Cut each steak across the grain into slices ½ inch (12 mm) thick. Fan the slices on warmed individual serving plates and pour the accumulated juices from the platter and carving board over the steaks. Pass the horseradish cream at the table. Serve at once.

2 boneless New York strip steaks, each about ¾ lb (375 g) and 1 inch (2.5 cm) thick

Extra-virgin olive oil

Kosher salt and freshly ground pepper

FOR THE HORSERADISH CREAM

½ cup (4 fl oz/125 ml) heavy (double) cream

2 tablespoons prepared horseradish

½ teaspoon Dijon mustard

Kosher salt

3 or 4 drops hot-pepper sauce

SERVES 2–4

Lamb loin chops vary in size, but you can count on two chops per person for light eaters and three chops for diners with heartier appetites. To keep the color vibrant, make the tangy, herb-flecked salsa verde no more than 3 to 4 hours in advance, or store it tightly covered and refrigerated for up to 12 hours.

━━━━━━━━━━━━━━

To make the salsa verde, in a mini food processor, pulse the garlic until minced. Add the parsley, mint, anchovy, capers, mustard, and vinegar, and pulse until smooth. Add the oil and pulse until evenly blended and thick. Cover and refrigerate for at least 1 hour to blend the flavors.

Remove the chops from the refrigerator and let stand at room temperature for 30 minutes. Preheat the oven to 250°F (120°C). Pat the chops dry with paper towels and season both sides generously with salt and pepper.

Place a large ovenproof frying pan over high heat, add the 2 teaspoons oil, and heat until it begins to shimmer, about 3 minutes. Add the butter and reduce the heat to medium-high. When the butter foams, add the chops without letting them touch. Sear until crusty and golden, about 2–2½ minutes on each side. Transfer the meat to a plate and, working with one at a time, lift each chop with tongs and sear all the fatty edges, about 45 seconds per chop.

Transfer the meat to the pan and roast until an instant-read thermometer inserted into a chop away from the bone registers 130°F (54°C) for medium-rare, 20–25 minutes, or until done to your liking. Transfer to a warmed serving platter and let rest for about 5 minutes. Top the chops with the salsa verde and serve right away.

PAN-ROASTED T-BONE LAMB CHOPS WITH SALSA VERDE

FOR THE SALSA VERDE

1 clove garlic

1¼ cups (1½ oz/45 g) firmly packed fresh flat-leaf parsley leaves

¼ cup (¼ oz/7 g) packed fresh mint leaves

1 anchovy fillet, packed in salt, soaked in warm water for 5 minutes then drained, and patted dry

1 tablespoon capers, rinsed

1 teaspoon Dijon mustard

1½ teaspoons white or red wine vinegar

⅓ cup (3 fl oz/80 ml) extra-virgin olive oil

8–12 bone-in T-bone or loin lamb chops, 2–2½ lb (1–1.25 kg) total weight

Kosher salt and freshly ground pepper

2 teaspoons olive oil

2 teaspoons unsalted butter

SERVES 4

Brilliant in color and spiced with mint, jalapeño, and tangerines, the relish is also great paired with roast turkey or pork. It would make a unique addition to the Thanksgiving table. Ask your butcher to "french" the racks by cutting the meat and fat from the rib ends. This makes a neater presentation if you are carving at the table and makes it easier to cut the racks into chops.

RACK OF LAMB WITH SPICY CRANBERRY RELISH

½ cup (4 fl oz/125 ml) fresh
tangerine juice

¼ cup (2 fl oz/60 ml) canola
or grapeseed oil

Kosher salt and freshly
ground pepper

3 racks of lamb, about 2½ lb
(1.25 kg) each, trimmed
and frenched

FOR THE RELISH

2 tangerines

1 cup (4 oz/125 g) fresh or
frozen cranberries

½ large white onion,
coarsely chopped

⅓ cup (3 fl oz/80 ml)
rice vinegar

¼ cup (¼ oz/7 g) packed
fresh mint leaves

1 small jalapeño chile,
coarsely chopped

3 tablespoons sugar,
or to taste

Pinch of kosher salt

SERVES 8–10

In a large, shallow dish, combine the tangerine juice and oil and season with salt and pepper. Add the lamb and turn to coat the racks on all sides. Let stand at room temperature for about 1 hour, turning occasionally.

Meanwhile, make the relish: Juice 1 of the tangerines and chop the other coarsely, skin and all, and remove any seeds. In a blender or food processor, combine the tangerine juice, chopped tangerine, cranberries, onion, vinegar, mint, and jalapeño and purée until smooth. Pour the mixture into a bowl and add the sugar and kosher salt. Let stand at room temperature for at least 30 minutes or up to 2 hours.

Preheat the oven to 450°F (230°C).

If desired, wrap the ends of the bones with aluminum foil to keep them from burning. Arrange the lamb racks, bone side down, in a roasting pan. Roast until an instant-read thermometer inserted into the center of the lamb away from the bone registers 130°F (54°C) for medium-rare, 15–20 minutes, or until done to your liking. Transfer the racks to a carving board and tent with aluminum foil. Let rest for 10–15 minutes.

Cut the racks between the bones into individual chops. Arrange 2 or 3 chops per person on warmed individual plates, with the relish alongside. Serve right away.

Figs have a fleeting season, but dried figs plump up nicely in warm liquid and can be used any time of year. Their sweet flavor is complemented by the tang of balsamic vinegar and the salt of prosciutto in a sauce made from the pan drippings. Serve with a simple green salad and buttered orzo or couscous.

BABY LAMB CHOPS WITH FIG-BALSAMIC PAN SAUCE

1 rack of lamb, about 2 lb (1 kg) and 8 ribs, chine bone removed, frenched, and trimmed of fat

Kosher salt and freshly ground pepper

1 tablespoon olive oil

2 teaspoons unsalted butter, plus 1 tablespoon for finishing the sauce (optional)

1 oz (30 g) prosciutto, finely chopped

2 large shallots, minced

⅓ cup (3 fl oz/80 ml) good-quality balsamic vinegar

4 dried figs, stems removed, finely chopped

¾ teaspoon minced fresh rosemary

1¾ cups (14 fl oz/430 ml) beef stock or low-sodium broth, simmered to reduce to about ½ cup (4 fl oz/125 ml)

SERVES 2–4

Cut midway between every second bone of the rack to yield 4 double-rib chops, or ask your butcher to do this for you. Pat the chops thoroughly dry and season both sides generously with salt and pepper. Let stand at room temperature for 30 minutes.

Preheat the oven to 225°F (110°C) and place a roasting pan inside the oven to heat.

Place a large, heavy frying pan over medium-high heat, add the oil, and heat until it begins to shimmer, about 2 minutes. Add the chops and sear until golden brown, about 2–2½ minutes on each side. Transfer the chops to a plate and, working with one at a time, lift each chop with tongs and sear all the fatty edges, about 1 minute per chop. Transfer the chops to the preheated roasting pan and roast until an instant-read thermometer inserted into the thickest part of a chop away from the bone registers 130°F (54°C) for medium-rare, 20–30 minutes, or until done to your liking. Let rest for about 3 minutes.

Meanwhile, discard any oil from the pan, and melt the 2 teaspoons butter over medium-low heat. Add the prosciutto and shallots, and cook until the shallots are softened and the prosciutto is golden, about 2 minutes. Add the vinegar, figs, and rosemary, raise the heat to medium, and deglaze the pan, scraping to remove any browned bits from the bottom of the pan. Cook until the liquid is reduced by about two-thirds, about 1½ minutes. Stir in the stock and a pinch of pepper. Bring to a simmer and cook for 1 minute. Remove from the heat and, if desired, stir in the 1 tablespoon butter until melted.

Arrange the chops on warmed individual plates, top with the sauce, and serve right away.

Lamb chops cook quickly in the high heat of the oven. This is a good recipe to keep in mind when you want something special and super-easy to pull off or if you your herb garden is proliferating. Use your favorite combination of chopped fresh herbs to customize the flavor, such as flat-leaf parsley, thyme, mint, marjoram, and rosemary.

HERB-CRUSTED LAMB CHOPS

Preheat the oven to 450°F (230°C).

Season the lamb chops on both sides with salt and pepper. Stir together the herbs, oil, mustard, and garlic. Spread the herb mixture all over the chops.

Place an oiled flat rack in a large roasting pan. Arrange the lamb chops on the rack and roast until an instant-read thermometer inserted into the thickest part of a chop away from bone registers 130°F (54°C) for medium-rare, 15–17 minutes, or until done to your liking. Remove from the oven and tent the chops with aluminum foil. Let rest for 5 minutes.

Serve right away.

12 lamb rib chops, 3½–4 lb (1.75–2 kg) total weight, trimmed

Kosher salt and freshly ground pepper

½ cup (½ oz/15 g) minced mixed fresh herbs

2 tablespoons extra-virgin olive oil

1 tablespoon Dijon mustard

2 cloves garlic, finely chopped

SERVES 6

These Moroccan-inspired lamb shanks call for a hybrid method of roasting: The lamb is browned at a high temperature, then the temperature is reduced, and the lamb is covered and slow-roasted to tenderize the tough connective tissue. Look for preserved lemons in specialty shops. Serve with couscous and a chopped vegetable salad.

In a small bowl, stir together the paprika, cumin, ginger, and 1 teaspoon salt. In a large bowl, sprinkle the mixture evenly over the lamb shanks. Cover, and let stand for 1 hour at room temperature or for up to 4 hours in the refrigerator. (If the lamb is refrigerated, remove it about 30 minutes before roasting.)

Preheat the oven to 450°F (230°C).

In a roasting pan just large enough to hold the shanks in a single layer, spread the onions to cover the bottom of the pan and sprinkle with the garlic. Place the shanks on the onions, drizzle with the oil, toss to coat, then spread out evenly. Roast until the shanks begin to brown, about 20 minutes. Remove the pan from the oven and reduce the oven temperature to 325°F (165°C).

Pour 1 cup (8 fl oz/250 ml) water around the shanks, then cover the pan tightly with a double layer of heavy-duty aluminum foil. Roast until the lamb is easily pierced with a fork, about 1½ hours.

Remove the pan from the oven, add the tomatoes and cilantro, and turn the shanks with tongs to distribute the ingredients. Raise the oven temperature to 375°F (190°C) and roast, uncovered, until the meat is almost falling off the bone, about 45 minutes.

Remove the pan from the oven and stir in the olives and preserved lemon. Let stand for 5 minutes to warm the olives. Transfer the shanks to a warmed platter or individual plates. Spoon the sauce and olives over the shanks. Serve right away.

SLOW-ROASTED LAMB SHANKS WITH OLIVES & PRESERVED LEMON

¾ teaspoon sweet paprika

½ teaspoon ground cumin

¼ teaspoon ground ginger

Kosher salt

6 lamb shanks, about 1 lb (16 oz) each

2 yellow onions, sliced

3 cloves garlic, minced

2 tablespoons extra-virgin olive oil

1 can (28 oz/875 g) diced tomatoes, with juices

½ cup (¾ oz/20 g) chopped fresh cilantro

1 cup (4 oz/125 g) pitted green olives

1 preserved lemon, peel only, chopped, or grated zest of 1 lemon

SERVES 6

Sautéing radicchio softens its bitter edge, mellows its vibrant color, and renders it a delicious partner to roasted lamb flavored with garlic and lemon.

LEG OF LAMB WITH SAUTÉED RADICCHIO

1 bone-in leg of lamb,
4–5 lb (2–2.5 kg),
trimmed of excess fat

3 tablespoons
minced garlic

Kosher salt and freshly
ground pepper

3 tablespoons olive oil

1 lemon, thinly sliced

¼ lb (125 g) thick-sliced
pancetta, diced

1 large head radicchio,
cored and thinly sliced

2 teaspoons minced
fresh rosemary

SERVES 6

Remove the lamb from the refrigerator and let stand at room temperature for about 1½ hours.

Preheat the oven to 500°F (260°C).

In a small bowl, combine the garlic, 1 tablespoon salt, 1½ teaspoons pepper, and 2 tablespoons of the oil. Mix well. Using a small, sharp knife, cut 10 slits about 1½ inches (4 cm) deep into the lamb. Push some of the garlic mixture into the slits and rub the rest all over the outside of the lamb.

Place a sheet of aluminum foil in a large roasting pan, shiny side down. Distribute the lemon slices evenly in the center. Place the lamb on the lemon slices. Roast for 20 minutes. Reduce the oven temperature to 300°F (150°C) and roast until an instant-read thermometer inserted into the thickest part of the lamb away from the bone registers 130°F (54°C) for medium-rare, 30–45 minutes more, or until done to your liking. Begin checking the temperature 20 minutes after reducing the heat. Transfer the lamb to a carving board and tent with aluminum foil. Let rest for 10–15 minutes.

Meanwhile, warm the remaining 1 tablespoon oil in a large, heavy frying pan over medium heat. Add the pancetta and cook, stirring occasionally, until lightly golden and crisp, 5–6 minutes. Stir in the radicchio and rosemary and cook until the radicchio is wilted and golden, 4–5 minutes more.

Cut the lamb across the grain into thin slices. Serve right away with the radicchio.

Plan ahead when making this recipe, as it needs to be refrigerated for 24 hours after applying the spice rub. The stuffing is simple, but the intrinsic sweetness of peppers and onions is a nice foil to the bold flavor of the meat.

LEG OF LAMB STUFFED WITH PEPPERS & ONIONS

1 boneless leg of lamb, about 5 lb (2.5 kg), trimmed

1 teaspoon granulated garlic

½ teaspoon ground cumin

Kosher salt and freshly ground pepper

2 tablespoons extra-virgin olive oil

2 tablespoons balsamic vinegar

FOR THE STUFFING

1 tablespoon extra-virgin olive oil

1 large yellow onion, sliced

2 red bell peppers, roasted, peeled, and seeded, then sliced

SERVES 8–10

Lay the roast out flat, boned side up. Cut shallow slashes into the thicker muscles to help the roast cook evenly. In a small bowl, stir together the garlic, cumin, 2 teaspoons salt, and ½ teaspoon pepper. On a large plate, rub the spice mixture all over the meat. Refrigerate, uncovered, for 24 hours.

About 2 hours before roasting, in a small bowl, stir together the oil and vinegar. Brush all over the meat. Return to the refrigerator. Remove the lamb from the refrigerator about 1 hour before roasting.

Meanwhile, make the stuffing: In a frying pan over medium heat, warm the oil. Add the onion and sauté until softened, 2–3 minutes. Add 2 tablespoons water, cover, reduce the heat to low, and cook until the onion is tender, 8–10 minutes. Do not brown. Remove the pan from the heat, uncover, and cool.

Preheat the oven to 375°F (190°C). Oil a flat roasting rack and place it in a roasting pan just large enough to hold the lamb.

Place the lamb on a work surface, boned side up. Place the bell peppers and onion in a line down the center of the length of the meat. Starting from a long side, roll the meat up tightly around the vegetables. Using kitchen string, tie the roll crosswise at regular intervals, forming a compact cylinder. Center a 30-inch (75-cm) long piece of kitchen string lengthwise under the roast. Place a 4-inch (10-cm) square of aluminum foil over each end of the roast to hold the stuffing in place, and tie the string securely, but not too tightly, around the roast. Roast the lamb until a thermometer inserted into the thickest part of the roll registers 130° (54°C) for medium-rare, about 1¼ hours, or until done to your liking.

Remove the pan from the oven, transfer the lamb to a carving board, and tent with aluminum foil. Let rest for 20 minutes. To serve, snip the strings and cut into thick slices.

Here, a hearty, yet easy-to-prepare, sausage and Parmesan stuffing flavors a boneless, butterflied leg of lamb from the inside. A light, simple pan sauce adds a welcome, tart balance to the finished dish.

LAMB SHOULDER WITH SAUSAGE, LEEK & ONION STUFFING

To make the stuffing, in a frying pan over medium heat, warm the oil. Remove the casing from the sausage and add the sausage and sauté until no longer pink, 6–7 minutes. Transfer to a cutting board. Finely chop the onion and the white and pale green parts of the leek. Add the leek and onion to the pan and cook until lightly golden, about 5 minutes. Stir in the thyme and garlic and cook for 1 minute more. Let cool for 5 minutes. Chop the sausage and add to the pan. Add the bread crumbs, Parmesan, and egg. Stir to mix thoroughly.

Preheat the oven to 450°F (230°C). Place a rack in a large roasting pan.

Lay the lamb, fat side down, on a work surface, with one narrow end facing you. Season generously with salt and pepper. Spread the stuffing over the lamb, leaving 3–4 inches (7.5–10 cm) uncovered at the far end. Beginning at the end closest to you, roll up the lamb tightly. Using kitchen string, tie the roll crosswise at regular intervals, forming a compact cylinder. Pat dry with paper towels. Brush with the oil and season generously with salt and pepper.

Transfer to the pan and roast for 25 minutes. Reduce the oven temperature to 325°F (165°C). Continue to roast until an instant-read thermometer inserted into the thickest part of the lamb registers 130°F (54°C) for medium-rare, about 30–40 minutes more, or until done to your liking. Transfer to a carving board and tent with aluminum foil. Let rest for 10–20 minutes.

Tip the roasting pan and spoon off a little fat, if desired. Pour the pan juices into a saucepan over medium-high heat and add the wine, stock, and lemon juice. Simmer briskly to reduce the liquid by about half, about 5 minutes. Stir in the dill. Taste and adjust the seasoning. Snip the strings from the lamb and carve into thick slices. Transfer to a warmed platter, drizzle with some of the herbed pan juices, and serve right away.

FOR THE STUFFING

1 tablespoon olive oil

1 sweet Italian sausage

1 small sweet onion

1 leek

1 tablespoon chopped fresh thyme

2 cloves garlic, minced

¾ cup (1½ oz/45 g) fresh bread crumbs

¼ cup (1 oz/30 g) grated Parmesan cheese

1 large egg, lightly beaten

1 boneless lamb shoulder, 3–3½ lb (1.5–1.75 kg), butterflied

Kosher salt and freshly ground pepper

1 tablespoon olive oil

½ cup (4 fl oz/125 ml) dry white wine

½ cup (4 fl oz/125 ml) chicken stock or low-sodium broth

Juice of 1 lemon

2 tablespoons chopped fresh dill or flat-leaf parsley

SERVES 6–8

One of the great reasons to serve a butterflied leg of lamb at a dinner party is that it produces a range of doneness levels—from rare to medium-well—due to its uneven thickness, so it will cater to the different tastes of your guests. If you are pressed for time, ask your butcher to butterfly the lamb.

To make the tapenade, in a food processor, combine the green and black olives, mint, oil, garlic, lemon zest, and brandy (if using). Season with pepper and pulse to form a very chunky purée. Set aside. Remove the lamb from the refrigerator and let stand at room temperature for 1–1½ hours.

Preheat the oven to 425°F (220°C).

On a work surface, lay the lamb with the fat side down and the "hinge" in the center. Arrange 4 lengths of kitchen string underneath the lamb so they extend 4–6 inches (10–15 cm) on either side. Rub most of the tapenade all over the lamb, poking it into all the nooks and crannies. Fold the lamb in half down the center as if closing a book. Tie the strings around the lamb crosswise at even intervals to secure the stuffing. Brush the lamb with oil and season generously with salt and pepper. Rub the remaining tapenade over the top.

Arrange the lamb on a rack in a roasting pan, transfer to the oven, and roast for 20 minutes. Reduce the oven temperature to 300°F (150°C) and continue to roast until an instant-read thermometer inserted into the thickest part of the lamb—not the stuffing—registers 130°F (54°C) for medium-rare, about 45 minutes, or until done to your liking. Transfer to a carving board and tent with aluminum foil. Let rest for 10 minutes.

Snip the strings and cut into thick slices. Serve right away with lemon wedges.

LEG OF LAMB STUFFED WITH LEMON-OLIVE TAPENADE

FOR THE TAPENADE

¾ cup (3½ oz/105 g) brine-cured mild green olives, such as Picholine or Lucques, pitted

¾ cup (3 oz/90 g) Kalamata olives, pitted

2 tablespoons coarsely chopped fresh mint

1 tablespoon lemon or plain extra-virgin olive oil

4 cloves garlic, sliced

Grated zest of 1 lemon

½ teaspoon brandy or Cognac (optional)

Freshly ground pepper

1 bone-in leg of lamb, 3½–4 lb (1.75–2 kg), butterflied (page 23), flattened, and trimmed of excess fat

Olive oil, for brushing

Kosher salt and freshly ground pepper

Lemon wedges, for serving

SERVES 6

Roasting meat on the bone adds extra flavor, and the bone helps conduct heat, so the meat cooks more rapidly than that of a boneless leg. Here, the leg is started at a high temperature, then a crust of yogurt and bread crumbs is applied, and the lamb finishes roasting at a moderate temperature.

LEG OF LAMB WITH BREAD CRUMB CRUST

1 bone-in, butt-end half leg of lamb, 4–5 lb (2–2.5 kg)

Extra-virgin olive oil, for coating

Kosher salt and freshly ground pepper

FOR THE TOPPING

1½ cups (3 oz/90 g) fresh bread crumbs

3 tablespoons plain yogurt

1 tablespoon extra-virgin olive oil

1 tablespoon finely chopped flat-leaf parsley

1 clove garlic, finely chopped

1 teaspoon herbes de Provence

SERVES 6

Remove the lamb from the refrigerator 1 hour before roasting. Preheat the oven to 425°F (220°C). Line a roasting pan just large enough to hold the lamb with heavy-duty aluminum foil. Oil a flat roasting rack and place it in the prepared pan.

Using a sharp knife, trim most of the surface fat from the lamb. Rub it all over with oil, and season generously with salt and pepper. Place the lamb, rounded side up, on the rack, and roast for 30 minutes.

Meanwhile, make the topping: In a small bowl, stir together the bread crumbs, yogurt, oil, parsley, garlic, and herbes de Provence until evenly moistened.

Remove the pan from the oven. Using a large spoon, firmly press the topping onto the rounded top of the leg. Reduce the oven temperature to 350°F (180°C) and continue to roast the lamb until an instant-read thermometer inserted into the thickest part away from the bone registers 130°F (54°C) for medium-rare, 50–60 minutes, or until done to your liking. Transfer the lamb to a carving board and tent with aluminum foil. Let rest for 15–20 minutes.

Carve the lamb and transfer the slices to a warmed platter or individual plates. If serving on individual plates, make sure that each portion includes some of the bread-crumb crust. Serve right away.

These tenderloins feature a crisp bread-crumb crust that is flavored with fennel seeds and dried herbs. They are easy to make, yet impressive enough to serve at a dinner party. Serve them with braised garlicky greens and Roasted Root Vegetable Medley (page 193).

FENNEL-CRUSTED PORK TENDERLOIN

In a shallow baking dish, rub the vinegar all over the tenderloins. In a small bowl, combine the fennel seeds, oregano, and thyme with 1 teaspoon salt and 1 teaspoon pepper. Rub each tenderloin all over with half of the seasoning mixture. Cover with plastic wrap and refrigerate for at least 4 hours or overnight.

Remove the tenderloins from the refrigerator and let stand at room temperature for 30 minutes. Preheat the oven to 400°F (200°C). Place a rack on a rimmed baking sheet.

In a small frying pan over low heat, warm the oil. Add the shallot and cook until softened but not brown, 4–5 minutes. Add the bread crumbs and garlic, raise the heat to medium-high, and cook, stirring, until the crumbs are toasted and fragrant, about 3 minutes. Let cool.

Transfer the crumb mixture to a platter, breaking up any clumps with a fork, and spread in an even layer. Roll each tenderloin in the bread-crumb mixture, pressing to help the mixture adhere firmly. Carefully transfer the tenderloins to the rack.

Roast until the crust is crisp and brown and an instant-read thermometer inserted into the thickest part of a tenderloin registers 135°F (57°C) for medium, about 25 minutes, or until done to your liking. Remove from the oven; transfer to a carving board and tent with aluminum foil. Let rest for 5 minutes. Cut each tenderloin crosswise into thick slices and serve right away.

2 pork tenderloins, 10–12 oz (315–375 g) each, silver skin removed and trimmed

2 teaspoons white vinegar

1 tablespoon coarsely crushed fennel seeds

½ teaspoon dried oregano

½ teaspoon dried thyme

Kosher salt and freshly ground pepper

2 tablespoons olive oil

1 large shallot, finely chopped

⅓ cup (1½ oz/45 g) fine dried bread crumbs

1 clove garlic, minced

SERVES 4

Mojo de ajo refers to Latin-style sauces that rely on garlic, or *ajo*, as a main flavoring agent. The garlic is often paired with tangy citrus juice that brightens up the flavors of the dish. Serve with steamed rice and black beans to complete the Latin theme.

CUBAN-STYLE PORK WITH MOJO DE AJO

1 teaspoon sweet paprika

Kosher salt and freshly ground pepper

2 pork tenderloins, about ¾ lb (375 g) each, silver skin removed, and trimmed

2 tablespoons extra-virgin olive oil

FOR THE MOJO DE AJO

¼ cup (2 fl oz/60 ml) extra-virgin olive oil

2 cloves garlic, chopped

2 tablespoons minced fresh flat-leaf parsley

½ teaspoon red pepper flakes

½ cup (4 fl oz/125 ml) fresh orange juice

Kosher salt

SERVES 4

In a small bowl, combine the paprika, 1 teaspoon salt, and ½ teaspoon pepper. Rub the paprika mixture all over the tenderloins. Transfer to a plate, cover, and let stand for 1 hour at room temperature.

Preheat the oven to 375°F (190°C).

In a large, heavy ovenproof frying pan over high heat, warm the 2 tablespoons oil. When the oil is shimmering, add the tenderloins and sear on all sides, about 5 minutes total. Transfer the pan to the oven and roast the pork until an instant-read thermometer inserted into the thickest part of a tenderloin registers 135°F (57°C) for medium, 30 minutes, or until done to your liking. Remove the pan from the oven, transfer the pork to a carving board, and tent with aluminum foil. Let rest for 10 minutes.

Meanwhile, make the sauce: In a small nonreactive frying pan over medium-low heat, warm the ¼ cup (2 fl oz/60 ml) oil. Add the garlic and cook, stirring often, until golden-brown, about 4 minutes. Stir in the parsley and pepper flakes and cook for 10 seconds. Add the orange juice and simmer, swirling the pan once or twice, until slightly reduced, about 2 minutes. Season to taste with salt and remove from heat.

Cut each tenderloin crosswise into thick slices. Arrange the slices on a warmed platter or individual plates. Spoon the sauce over the pork and serve right away.

This dish comes together quickly and is a perfect weeknight meal. The pork is flavored simply with a two-ingredient glaze, then cooked in a hot oven. While it roasts, you'll have time to make an easy fruit compote to serve alongside the sliced meat.

PORK WITH APPLE-GINGER COMPOTE

2 pork tenderloins, 1–1¼ lb (500–625 g) each, silver skin removed, and trimmed

Kosher salt and freshly ground pepper

2 tablespoons apricot jam

2 tablespoons Dijon mustard

FOR THE COMPOTE:

2 tablespoons unsalted butter

1 large yellow onion

Kosher salt

2 Granny Smith or other tart green apples

⅓ cup (2 oz/60 g) golden raisins

2 tablespoons apricot jam

1 teaspoon peeled and grated fresh ginger

½ teaspoon dry mustard

4 drops hot-pepper sauce

Dash of ground white pepper

½ cup (4 fl oz/125 ml) dry white wine

SERVES 4–6

Preheat the oven to 425°F (220°C). Line a roasting pan with aluminum foil. Oil a rack large enough to hold the tenderloins and place the rack in the pan.

Generously season the tenderloins with salt and pepper. In a small bowl, whisk together the apricot jam and mustard. Brush the mixture all over the tenderloins, then place them on the rack. Roast until an instant-read thermometer inserted into the thickest part of a tenderloin registers 135°F (57°C) for medium, 30–35 minutes, or until done to your liking. Remove the pan from the oven, transfer the tenderloins to a carving board, and tent with aluminum foil. Let rest for 10 minutes.

Meanwhile, make the compote: In a frying pan over medium heat, melt the butter. Thinly slice the onion and add the onion and ¼ teaspoon salt and sauté until the onion is lightly golden, 8–10 minutes. Peel and dice the apples. Add the apples, raisins, jam, ginger, mustard, hot-pepper sauce, and white pepper and stir to combine. Pour in the wine, bring to a boil, then reduce the heat to low. Cover and simmer, stirring occasionally, until the apples are soft, about 10 minutes. If the mixture is too thin, uncover and continue to cook for a few minutes until it has reduced and thickened. Transfer the compote to a serving bowl and serve warm or at room temperature.

To serve, cut the tenderloins on the diagonal into thick slices and season with salt. Serve right away, passing the compote at the table.

Onions simmered with butter, brown sugar, balsamic vinegar, and golden raisins create an easy topping for roasted pork tenderloins that is reminiscent of what you might find in the southern part of Italy.

PORK WITH SWEET & SOUR ONIONS

Preheat the oven to 375°F (190°C).

In a large frying pan over medium heat, melt the butter. Add the onions and sauté until softened, about 2 minutes. Stir in the raisins, brown sugar, vinegar, and salt and pepper to taste and cook until the onions are tender and glazed, about 3 minutes.

Arrange the pork tenderloins in an oiled roasting pan just large enough to hold them comfortably. Spoon the onion mixture over the pork. Roast the pork until browned on the outside and an instant-read thermometer inserted into the thickest part of a tenderloin registers 135°F (57°C) for medium, about 45 minutes, or until done to your liking.

Remove the pan from the oven, transfer the pork tenderloins to a carving board, and tent with aluminum foil. Let rest for 5 minutes. To serve, cut the tenderloins on the diagonal into thick slices. Serve right away on warmed individual plates with the onions.

2 tablespoons unsalted butter

2 large Vidalia or other sweet onions, sliced

1/2 cup (3 oz/90 g) golden raisins

2 tablespoons firmly packed dark brown sugar

2 tablespoons balsamic vinegar

Kosher salt and freshly ground pepper

2 pork tenderloins, about 1 lb (500 g) each, silver skin removed, and trimmed

SERVES 8

This savory roast is a variation on Italian-style porchetta. It is dry-brined for two days before roasting (be sure to plan ahead), so it emerges from the oven tender and juicy. The roast is just as delicious at room temperature as it is warm, so it's a great make-ahead dish for a casual dinner party.

HERB-STUFFED PORK LOIN

1 tablespoon peppercorns

1 tablespoon coriander seeds

4 bay leaves, torn

Kosher salt and freshly ground pepper

1 boneless pork loin, 4½–6 lb (2.25–3 kg), trimmed and butterflied

10 cloves garlic

2 tablespoons fennel seeds

1 tablespoon minced fresh rosemary

1 tablespoon minced fresh sage

Grated zest of 2 lemons

3 tablespoons olive oil, plus extra for brushing

SERVES 8–10

Bruise the peppercorns, coriander, and bay leaves slightly in a mortar with a pestle, or pulse a few times in a mini food processor. Transfer to a bowl. Stir in ¾ teaspoon salt for each pound (500 g) of meat. On a large rimmed platter, rub the spice mixture all over the pork, concentrating it on the thicker parts. Cover and refrigerate the pork for 48 hours.

Remove the pork from the refrigerator and rinse briefly under cold running water to remove the spice mixture. Pat dry with paper towels. Let stand at room temperature for 1½ hours.

Preheat the oven to 450°F (230°C).

In a mini food processor, pulse the garlic until finely chopped. Add the fennel seeds, rosemary, sage, lemon zest, and the 3 tablespoons oil. Add ½ teaspoon salt and several grinds of pepper. Pulse to form a paste. Spread the paste over the inside of the pork, then roll the meat into a cylinder about 4 inches (10 cm) in diameter. Using kitchen string, tie the roll crosswise at regular intervals, forming a compact cylinder. Pat the pork dry using paper towels. In a roasting pan, brush the pork with oil and sprinkle generously with pepper.

Transfer to the oven and roast for 30 minutes. Reduce the temperature to 325°F (165°C) and roast until an instant-read thermometer inserted into the thickest part of the roast registers 135°F (57°C) for medium, 20–25 minutes, or until done to your liking. Transfer the meat to a carving board and tent with aluminum foil. Let rest for 15–30 minutes.

To serve, snip the strings and cut crosswise into thick slices. Serve right away.

These pork chops are soaked for a few hours in a brine flavored with fresh lime and chile to make them moist and flavorful. They are then seared on the stove top and briefly roasted in a hot oven. Dark rum, allspice, lime juice, and hot-pepper sauce are all typical flavorings in the Caribbean.

CARIBBEAN-STYLE BRINED PORK CHOPS

To make the brine, in a large nonreactive bowl, combine ¼ cup (2 oz/60 g) salt with the brown sugar and 5 cups (40 fl oz/ 1.25 l) room-temperature water and stir until the salt and brown sugar dissolve. Add the allspice, peppercorns, and chile. Squeeze the lime juice into the bowl, and add the hollow halves; stir to mix. Add the pork chops, adding water as needed to ensure the brine covers the meat. Cover and refrigerate for 3–4 hours.

Preheat the oven to 450°F (230°C).

In a small bowl, make a basting sauce: Stir together the rum, brown sugar, lime zest and juice, and 2–3 drops hot-pepper sauce. Season to taste with salt and pepper. Set aside.

Remove the chops from the refrigerator about 30 minutes before roasting. Rinse them briefly under running cold water and pat dry with paper towels. Rub the chops on both sides with the oil. Warm a large heavy ovenproof frying pan over high heat until shimmering. Add the chops and sear for 2 minutes on each side. Brush with the basting sauce and transfer the pan to the oven. Roast until an instant-read thermometer inserted into the center of the meat away from the bone registers 135°F (57°C) for medium, 6–8 minutes, or until done to your liking.

Transfer the chops to warmed individual plates. Pour the remaining basting sauce into the pan and stir to scrape up the brown bits on the bottom of the pan. Bring to a boil and cook for 1 minute. Spoon the sauce over the chops, dividing evenly, and serve right away.

FOR THE BRINE

Kosher salt

¼ cup (2 oz/60 g) firmly packed golden brown sugar

8 whole allspice, lightly crushed

8 peppercorns

1 serrano chile, quartered lengthwise

1 lime, halved

4 bone-in pork chops, each about 10–12 oz (315–375 g)

2 tablespoons dark rum

2 teaspoons firmly packed golden brown sugar

Grated zest and juice of 1 lime

Hot-pepper sauce

Kosher salt and freshly ground pepper

2 teaspoons grapeseed oil

SERVES 4

More than any other type of meat, pork works well with a variety of fruits. Here, dried apricots and raisins are key flavors in a stuffing that is spread on a butterflied pork loin before it is rolled, tied, and roasted.

APRICOT-STUFFED PORK LOIN

In a bowl, mix together the apricots, raisins, and brandy. Let stand for 30 minutes. Drain the fruits, transferring them back to the bowl. Reserve the brandy. In a small frying pan over medium heat, warm 1 teaspoon of the oil. Add the shallots and sauté until lightly browned, 3–4 minutes. Add the vinegar, cook for 1 minute, then stir into the apricot mixture.

Preheat the oven to 350°F (180°C).

Place the pork loin, fat side down, on a cutting board. Spread the meat with the mustard and season with salt and pepper. Spread half the apricot mixture over the center third of the meat. Fold one third of the meat over the filling. Cover the top of this third with the remaining apricot mixture, and bring the remaining third of the meat over the top of the filling to make a roll. Using kitchen string, tie the roll crosswise at regular intervals, forming a compact cylinder. Tie a long string lengthwise around the roll.

Heat a large, heavy ovenproof frying pan over high heat until very hot. Add the remaining 2 teaspoons oil. Sear the pork loin until nicely browned, about 2 minutes. Turn the meat over and transfer the pan to the oven.

Roast the pork until an instant-read thermometer inserted into the thickest part of the loin registers 135°F (57°C) for medium, 1–1¼ hours, or until done to your liking. Transfer the pork to a carving board and tent with aluminum foil.

Carefully spoon off as much fat as possible from the pan. Pour the broth and the reserved brandy into the pan, bring to a boil over high heat, and boil for 5–10 minutes to reduce the volume slightly. Season to taste with salt and pepper.

To serve, snip the strings and cut crosswise into thick slices. Arrange on warmed plates, spoon a little of the juices on top, and serve right away. Pass the remaining juices in a warmed bowl at the table.

½ cup (3 oz/90 g) dried apricots, finely chopped

⅓ cup (2 oz/60 g) golden raisins

3 tablespoons brandy

3 teaspoons olive oil

½ cup (2 oz/60 g) thinly sliced shallots

1 teaspoon sherry vinegar

1 boneless center-cut pork loin roast, about 3 lb (1.5 kg), butterflied (see page 23)

1 tablespoon Dijon mustard

Kosher salt and freshly ground pepper

1¾ cups (14 fl oz/430 ml) chicken stock or low-sodium broth

SERVES 6

This is a great dish for a Sunday supper with family, as it's essentially a one-pot meal. The pork is seasoned simply with a quick 3-ingredient rub, then roasted along with a classic provençal combination of tomatoes, eggplant, sweet peppers, and summer squash. Serve the pork and vegetables with soft polenta or crusty bread to round out the meal.

HERB-RUBBED PORK LOIN WITH RATATOUILLE

FOR THE HERB RUB

½ teaspoon dried oregano

½ teaspoon garlic powder

Freshly ground pepper

1 boneless pork loin roast, about 3 lb (1.5 kg)

3 tomatoes, coarsely chopped

3 baby eggplants, peeled and diced

1 zucchini, diced

1 red or green bell pepper, seeded and diced

1 yellow onion, diced

2 tablespoons capers, including brine

3 cloves garlic, minced

2 teaspoons minced fresh basil or 1 teaspoon dried

Kosher salt and freshly ground pepper

SERVES 6

Preheat the oven to 400°F (200°C).

To make the spice rub, in a small bowl, combine the oregano, garlic powder, and pepper.

Pat the pork dry with paper towels and rub all over with the spice mixture. Place the pork in an oiled heavy roasting pan just large enough to hold it comfortably.

Arrange the tomato, eggplant, zucchini, bell pepper, and onion around the pork. Sprinkle with the capers, garlic, and basil, and season generously with salt and pepper. Roast the pork, stirring the vegetables every 30 minutes, until an instant-read thermometer inserted into the thickest part of the pork registers 135°F (57°C) for medium, about 1½ hours, or until done to your liking. Turn the vegetables twice during roasting.

Transfer the pork to a carving board and tent with aluminum foil. Let rest for 10 minutes. To serve, cut crosswise into thick slices and arrange on a warmed platter. Surround with the vegetables and serve right away.

For this fennel-and herb-scented pork roast, the garlic must be very finely minced—practically puréed—before being mixed with the rosemary mixture so that it does not scorch during roasting. Ask your butcher to remove the chine bone for easier carving. Accompany the pork and fennel wedges with the Fingerling Potatoes with Garlic & Thyme (page 183).

TUSCAN-STYLE PORK ROAST WITH FENNEL

In a spice grinder, process the rosemary, sea salt, and fennel seeds until finely ground. Transfer to a small bowl and stir in the garlic. Using a sharp knife, make several slashes on top of the roast, cutting through the fat but not into the meat. Rub 1 tablespoon oil all over the roast, then rub with the rosemary mixture and several grinds of pepper. Place the roast on a plate and cover loosely with plastic wrap. Refrigerate for 3 hours. Remove the roast about 30 minutes before roasting.

Preheat the oven to 375°F (190°C). Line a large rimmed baking sheet with heavy-duty aluminum foil.

Trim off the stems from each fennel bulb, reserving some of the fronds, then trim away any bruised outer leaves. Halve the fennel bulbs and onion lengthwise, then cut each half into 6 wedges. Transfer to a bowl, drizzle with the remaining 1 tablespoon olive oil, and sprinkle with kosher salt. Chop the reserved fennel fronds and add to the vegetables, tossing well.

Place the roast, bone side down, on the prepared baking sheet, surrounding it with the vegetables. Transfer to the oven and roast for 50 minutes. Carefully stir the vegetables and continue to roast until an instant-read thermometer inserted into the thickest part of the meat away from the bone registers 135°F (57°C) for medium, 10–20 minutes longer, or until done to your liking. Remove the pan from the oven. Transfer the roast to a carving board and tent with aluminum foil. Let rest for 10 minutes.

Cut between the bones to separate the roast into chops. Divide among warmed individual plates and spoon roasted vegetables alongside each chop. Serve right away.

1 tablespoon chopped fresh rosemary

1½ teaspoons coarse sea salt

¾ teaspoon fennel seeds

2 cloves garlic, very finely minced or pressed

One 6-rib bone-in pork loin roast, about 3½ lb (1.75 kg), tied

2 tablespoons extra-virgin olive oil

Kosher salt and freshly ground pepper

3 fennel bulbs

1 large yellow onion

SERVES 6

This dish is inspired by the flavors of the Mediterranean. Be sure to plan ahead when you want to make this recipe, as the garlicky fennel-and-lavender spice paste needs to soak into the meat for 24 to 48 hours prior to roasting. A second flavoring paste made from capers and lemon zest helps brighten the flavors.

BONE-IN PORK LOIN WITH MEDITERRANEAN FLAVORS

1½ teaspoons fennel seeds

1 teaspoon dried thyme

1 teaspoon dried lavender

Kosher salt and freshly ground pepper

4 cloves garlic, minced

2 tablespoons olive oil

1 rack of pork, about 6½ lb (3.25 kg) and 6 ribs

2 tablespoons capers, rinsed

Grated zest of 2 lemons

SERVES 6

In a mini food processor, combine the fennel seeds, thyme, and lavender. Pulse to blend and break up the seeds. Transfer to a small bowl and stir in 2 teaspoons salt, ¼ teaspoon pepper, the garlic, and 1 tablespoon oil to form a paste. Rub the paste all over the pork, concentrating the paste on the thicker, meaty side of the rack. Transfer to a baking dish, cover loosely, and refrigerate for at least 24 hours or preferably 48 hours.

Remove the pork from the refrigerator and let stand at room temperature for 30 minutes. Preheat the oven to 250°F (120°C). Line a rimmed baking sheet with aluminum foil.

In the food processor, combine the capers, lemon zest, and the remaining 1 tablespoon oil. Pulse until finely ground, scraping down the bowl once or twice.

Place the rack, bone side down, on the baking sheet. Rub the caper-lemon mixture over the top of the rack. Transfer to the oven and roast until an instant-read thermometer inserted into the thickest part of the pork registers 135°F (57°C) 1½–1¾ hours. Raise the oven temperature to 425°F (220°C) and continue to roast until the internal temperature reaches 140°F (60°C), about 20 minutes more. Transfer the rack to a carving board and tent with aluminum foil. Let rest for 10–15 minutes. Cut between the bones to separate the loin into chops and serve right away.

Chinese cuisine embraces and celebrates pork shoulder, whose rich meat is nicely offset by sweet, sour, and salty ingredients common to the food culture. This richly marbled cut stands up beautifully to the dry-heat method of roasting, but requires a relatively low heat and long roasting time to become fork-tender.

FIVE-SPICE PORK SHOULDER WITH GREEN ONION SALSA

Let the pork stand at room temperature for 1–1½ hours.

Preheat the oven to 425°F (220°C).

In a small bowl, stir together the five-spice powder, garlic, 2 teaspoons salt, and 1 teaspoon pepper. In a large shallow dish, rub the spice mixture all over the pork, then arrange the pork on a rack set over a roasting pan.

Transfer to the oven and roast for 45 minutes. Reduce the temperature to 350°F (180°C) and continue to roast until an instant-read thermometer inserted into the thickest part of the meat away from the bone registers 135°F (57°C) for medium, about 45 minutes longer, or until done to your liking. Let rest for about 30 minutes.

To prepare the salsa, in a medium bowl, stir together the green onions, vinegar, sherry, fish sauce, cilantro, soy sauce, sesame oil, and lemon juice.

Cut the pork into thick slices. Arrange on a warmed serving platter, top with the salsa, and serve right away.

1 bone-in pork shoulder, 5½–6 lb (2.75–3 kg)

2 teaspoons five-spice powder

3 cloves garlic, very finely minced or pressed

Kosher salt and freshly ground pepper

FOR THE SALSA

4 green onions, white and light green parts only, minced

4 teaspoons rice vinegar

4 teaspoons medium-dry sherry

4 teaspoons Asian fish sauce

2 teaspoons minced fresh cilantro

2 teaspoons reduced-sodium soy sauce

1 teaspoon Asian sesame oil

1 teaspoon fresh lemon juice

SERVES 4–6

When grilling season is months away, and you're craving barbecue pork ribs, turn to this recipe, which is made from start to finish in the oven. A homemade Kansas City–style barbecue sauce comes together quickly from pantry ingredients and is used as both a glaze and a table sauce. Round out the meal with corn bread and coleslaw.

BARBECUE-STYLE BABY BACK RIBS

FOR THE BARBECUE SAUCE

3 tablespoons peanut oil

1 yellow onion, chopped

4 cloves garlic, minced

1 jalapeño chile, seeded and sliced

1½ cups (9 oz/280 g) canned diced tomatoes, including juices

¼ cup (2 oz/60 g) firmly packed golden brown sugar

¼ cup (2 fl oz/60 ml) red wine vinegar

1 teaspoon Worcestershire sauce

1 teaspoon ground cumin

Kosher salt

6 lb (3 kg) baby back ribs, in slabs

SERVES 6

To make the barbecue sauce, in a saucepan over medium heat, heat the peanut oil. Add the onion, garlic, and chile and sauté until the onion is translucent, about 5 minutes. Add the tomatoes and their juices, brown sugar, vinegar, Worcestershire sauce, cumin, and ¼ teaspoon salt. Bring to a boil over medium heat, reduce the heat to low, and simmer, stirring occasionally, for 5 minutes to blend the flavors. Taste and adjust the seasoning. Let cool.

Preheat the oven to 350°F (180°C).

On a cutting board, cut the ribs into 6–8 rib sections and transfer the ribs to a rack in a roasting pan large enough to hold them comfortably, stacking them if needed. Pour 2 cups (16 fl oz/ 500 ml) water into the pan and cover tightly with heavy-duty aluminum foil. Bake the ribs for 45 minutes. Brush the ribs all over with the sauce and roast, uncovered, until fork-tender, about 15 minutes. Brush the ribs generously with sauce on both sides and tent with aluminum foil. Let rest for 5 minutes.

Serve right away, passing the remaining sauce at the table.

POULTRY

CHICKEN

ROASTED CHICKEN
WITH ONION SAUCE 86

CHICKEN BREASTS
WITH VEGETABLES
& WHITE WINE 87

MUSHROOM & RICOTTA–
STUFFED CHICKEN
BREASTS 88

PAN-ROASTED CHICKEN
LEGS WITH HERBED
PAN SAUCE 91

TANDOORI-STYLE
CHICKEN LEGS 92

CHICKEN THIGHS WITH
CHERRY COMPOTE 93

HERB & GARLIC CHICKEN 94

CRISP-SKINNED
BUTTERFLIED CHICKEN 96

CRISP CHICKEN WITH
TRUFFLE BUTTER 97

BUTTERFLIED CHICKEN
WITH LEMONS 99

CHILE-LIME CHICKEN 100

CHICKEN WITH HERBED
BREAD STUFFING 101

TURKEY

TURKEY BREASTS WITH
LEMON-PARSLEY GRAVY 104

TURKEY BREAST WITH
PROVENÇAL FLAVORS 106

SAGE-RUBBED TURKEY 108

BRINED TURKEY WITH
CORNBREAD & SAUSAGE
DRESSING 111

MAPLE-MUSTARD
TURKEY TENDERLOINS
WITH CRANBERRY-GINGER
RELISH 113

TURKEY WITH ROASTED
GARLIC & PARSLEY 114

DUCK & GOOSE

BALSAMIC DUCK LEGS
WITH MUSHROOMS

PAN-ROASTED DUCK
BREASTS WITH
DRIED-CHERRY SAUCE

POMEGRANATE-GLAZED
DUCK 120

CHRISTMAS GOOSE WITH
APPLE–DRIED FRUIT
COMPOTE 122

POULTRY FOR ROASTING

ng works well for a wide range of poultry. Whole birds
rticularly suited to roasting and can be prepared in
ty of ways, but poultry parts are good candidates for
ig, too, especially when you don't have a lot of time
oare a meal. Whether you purchase a whole bird or
ook for meaty, plump poultry with no visible blemishes
sing. Fresh poultry offers superior flavor and texture
ozen. If you do choose a frozen bird, thaw it overnight
refrigerator (never at room temperature) to ensure the
y stays wholesome.

t law prohibits the use of hormones and growth
ants in the poultry industry, but the labeling of poultry
nsistent and varies from processor to processor. To
quality and wholesomeness, seek out poultry from
ed local butcher and ask him or her to direct you

WHOLE BIRDS

CHOOSING Whole chickens were once labeled by the type of cooking method that was best suited to them, but the practice of labeling chickens as "roasters" or "broiler-fryers" is less common these days. More relevant to today's home cook is the weight of the bird. When planning a meal, allow about 1 pound (500 g) per person, as the bones add inedible weight.

PREPPING Despite popular practice, rinsing poultry before roasting is not necessary unless the bird has been brined. In fact, rinsing increases the chances of spreading bacteria that may be present on the bird. If present, remove the giblets from the bird's cavity and use poultry shears to remove any excess pieces of fat. Pat the birds dry with paper towels.

STORING Purchase whole birds as close as you can to roasting them. Keep up to 2 days in the refrigerator, or 3 months in the freezer before cooking. Thaw whole birds in the refrigerator overnight, which is the safest way to do it.

POULTRY PARTS

CHOOSING Look for poultry parts that appear meaty and plump with clear skin and no sign of feathers. Skin color is not necessarily an indication of quality when buying poultry. Color is a product of diet, so skin with a yellow hue indicates that yellow ingredients were included in the bird feed.

PREPPING Unless you are marinating them, pat the poultry parts dry with paper towels to encourage browning. Remove excess fat and skin with poultry shears. For the best value, buy a whole bird and cut it into parts yourself (see page 83).

STORING Purchase poultry parts as close as you can to roasting. Keep up to 2 days in the refrigerator, or 3 months in the freezer before cooking. Thaw in the refrigerator overnight.

OTHER POULTRY

CHOOSING For duck and geese, look for smooth, even skin and dark red meat. Patronize a reliable butcher shop for these less common birds, which may need to be special ordered.

PREPPING Thaw frozen birds in the refrigerator for 1 day. Remove the giblets and any lumps of fat from the cavity before cooking a whole duck or goose. Trim away any excess fat from duck breasts or legs.

STORING Store fresh birds for up to 2 days in the refrigerator. Store frozen birds for up to 3 months. Thaw frozen duck or goose in the refrigerator overnight before using.

TESTING POULTRY FOR DONENESS

Poultry parts can be tested by inserting the tip of a knife into a meaty section, ideally a joint. If the released juices run clear, not pink, the poultry is done. However, temperature is the most reliable test of doneness. Insert an instant-read thermometer into the thickest part of the poultry, without touching bone; when done, it should reach 170°F (77°C). One exception is boneless duck breast, which has dark, meatlike flesh and is best cooked to medium-rare (130–135°F/54°–57°C).

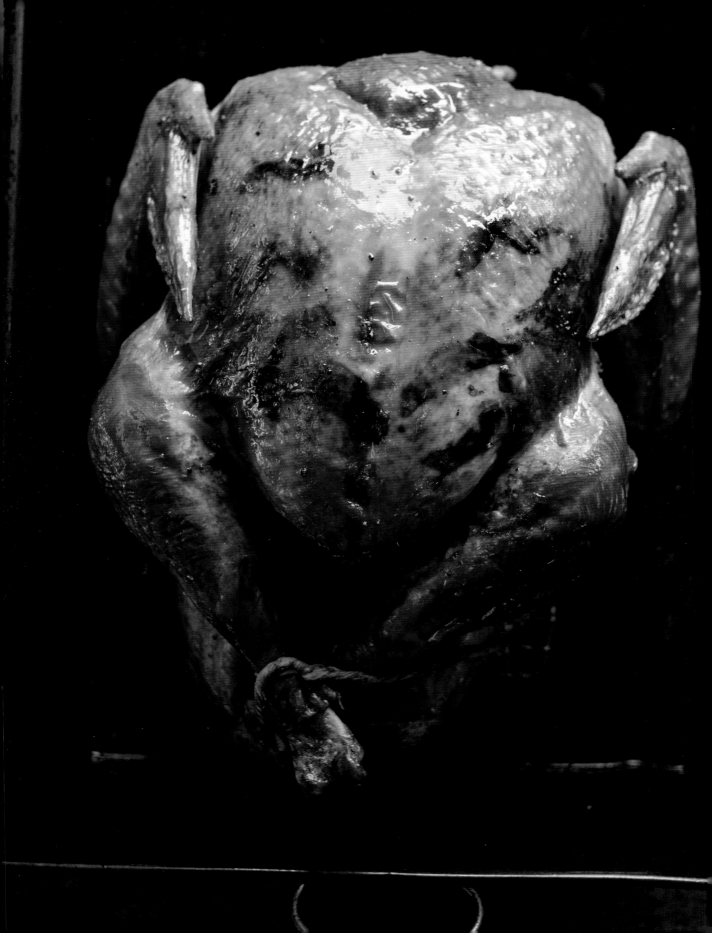

HOW TO ROAST POULTRY

1 PREP

Pat dry the whole bird or parts with paper towels. Trim them as directed, and bring just to room temperature (about 20 minutes for parts, 30 minutes for a whole chicken, or as directed in the recipe for larger birds). Preheat the oven to the desired temperature.

2 FLAVOR

Flavor the poultry with simple seasonings, such as flavored butter rubbed under the skin, or a rub, marinade, or brine. If a long soak is needed, you'll want to bring the bird to room temperature and preheat the oven afterwards (see Step 1). If you're using a stuffing, be sure it is completely cooled before adding it to the poultry cavity and be careful not to pack it too tightly.

3 BROWN

Some recipes, especially those calling for parts, may call for browning before the poultry goes into the oven. Be sure to choose a sturdy, ovenproof pan that can withstand high heat.

4 ROAST

Transfer the poultry to the oven and let it roast, paying attention to the cues in the recipe for turning or basting as needed.

5 CHECK

Test the poultry for doneness using an instant-read thermometer. For an accurate reading, insert the thermometer into the thickest part of the bird, not touching any bones.

6 REST

Be sure to let the poultry rest for 5–15 minutes, depending on the size. During this time, the meat will continue to cook a bit, while the juices are being reabsorbed throughout.

7 FINISH

Depending on how they are flavored, some poultry can be served immediately after resting, but others may benefit from a sauce made from the pan drippings. Follow the cues in the recipe.

BUTTERFYLING A WHOLE BIRD

Cutting out the backbone of a chicken so that it lies flat helps the bird cook more quickly and helps encourage evenly crisp skin.

1 ARRANGE ON A BOARD

Lay the chicken, breast side down, on a sturdy cutting board with the drumsticks pointing toward you.

2 REMOVE THE BACKBONE

Grip the chicken's tail (the pointy flap at the bottom). Using poultry shears or sharp kitchen shears, cut up along each side of the backbone, cutting all the way through. Remove the backbone and discard (or save for making stock).

3 FLATTEN THE BIRD

Turn the chicken over and push down on it between the breasts until the sternum breaks. Continue to push until the chicken is flattened, or butterflied.

TRUSSING A WHOLE BIRD

Trussing helps a whole bird cook evenly and helps the bird maintain a uniform shape. In some cases, tying the legs together also helps hold a stuffing inside the bird's cavity.

1 SECURE THE WINGS

Tuck the wing tips under the breast to keep them in place and prevent the wing tips from burning.

2 MAKE A COMPACT SHAPE

Using your hands, press the body of the bird together to form an even shape.

3 TIE THE LEGS TOGETHER

Cross the drumsticks and, using kitchen string, tie their bony ends together securely.

CUTTING UP A WHOLE CHICKEN

Buying a whole chicken and then cutting it into parts at home
is cost efficient. It's a good practice for small households,
as any unused parts can be saved for another meal.

1 REMOVE THE LEGS

Place the chicken breast side up. Pull a leg away from the body and, using poultry shears, cut through the thigh joint to remove the whole leg-thigh portion. Repeat to remove the other leg.

2 SEPARATE THE LEG PARTS

Locate the joint between the thigh and drumstick. Holding a leg securely, use the shears to cut through the joint to separate the parts. Repeat with the second leg.

3 REMOVE THE WINGS

Grasp a wing and pull it away from the body. Use the shears to cut through the joint to remove the wing. Repeat with the second wing.

4 REMOVE THE BACK

Turn the chicken over. Cut along one side of the backbone, from the body cavity to the neck cavity. Then cut along the other side and remove the back. Save the back for making stock, or discard it.

5 HALVE THE BREAST

Using the poultry shears, cut the breast lengthwise into halves. After cutting up the chicken, you will have a total of 8 pieces, plus the back.

CARVING A WHOLE BIRD

Carving a whole bird at the table is a holiday ritual. It's easier than many people think, especially if you divide the practice into these three distinct steps. There are two ways to handle the breast: either carve it directly form the bird, or remove the whole breast and cut it into neat slices.

1 REMOVE THE LEGS

Place the bird breast-side up on a carving board with the legs facing you. Using a carving knife, cut through the skin between the breast and thigh. Locate the thigh joint and cut through it to remove the drumstick. Repeat on the other side. Leave the thighs on the bird to stabilize it while you remove the breast.

2A CARVE THE BREAST

Just above the thigh and wing, carve a deep horizontal cut through the breast to the bone to create a base cut. Beginning at the breastbone, make a series of cuts downward and parallel to the rib cage, carving the meat from one side of the breast in long, thin slices. Repeat on the other side.

2B REMOVE THE BREAST & SLICE

You can also remove a breast half from the bone by cutting down along the breastbone to meet the horizontal cut. Place the breast half flat on a cutting surface and slice it crosswise to cut into medallions. Repeat on the other side.

3 REMOVE THE THIGHS & WINGS

Pry each thigh from the joint; then, use the knife to remove the thighs. Locate the joint between each wing and the breastbone and cut through the joints to remove the wings.

Here, onions roast alongside bone-in chicken breasts. The enriched onions are puréed for a satisfying, yet low-fat, sauce.

ROASTED CHICKEN WITH ONION SAUCE

2 tablespoons extra-virgin olive oil, plus more for greasing

4 bone-in, skin-on chicken breast halves, about 10 oz (315 g) each

1 tablespoon minced fresh rosemary

Kosher salt and freshly ground pepper

2 large sweet onions, quartered

¼ cup (2 fl oz/60 ml) dry sherry

¾ cup (6 fl oz/180 ml) chicken stock or low-sodium broth

SERVES 4

Preheat the oven to 425°F (220°C). Lightly brush a large roasting pan with oil.

Brush the skin of the chicken with 1 tablespoon oil. In a small bowl, combine the rosemary with 2 teaspoons salt and ½ teaspoon pepper. Arrange the chicken breasts skin side up in a single layer in the center of the prepared pan. Sprinkle with the rosemary mixture. In a large bowl, toss the onions with the remaining 1 tablespoon oil and ½ teaspoon each salt and pepper. Arrange the onions around the edges of the roasting pan.

Roast, stirring the onions occasionally, until the skin is browned and an instant-read thermometer inserted into the thickest part of a breast registers 170°F (77°C), about 35 minutes. Transfer the chicken to a serving platter and let rest for 10 minutes.

Raise the oven temperature to 475°F (245°C), and continue roasting the onions until very tender and darkened, about 5 minutes longer. Transfer the onions and any pan juices to a food processor. Place the roasting pan on the stove top over medium-high heat. Add the sherry and stock and bring to a boil, scraping up the browned bits from the bottom of the pan. Boil until the liquid is reduced to ¾ cup (6 fl oz/180 ml), about 2 minutes. Remove from the heat.

Process the onions, adding as much of the reduced liquid as needed to make a pourable sauce. Season to taste with salt and pepper. Pour some of the sauce over the chicken, and serve right away. Pass the remaining sauce at the table.

To ensure that all the vegetables cook evenly, the firmer ones are boiled briefly before roasting. Any uniformly cut vegetables can be substituted.

Pat the chicken breasts dry with paper towels. In a large nonreactive dish, stir together 3 tablespoons of the olive oil with the lemon zest and juice, and the red pepper flakes. Season to taste with salt and pepper. Add the chicken breasts to the marinade, turn to coat, cover, and refrigerate for 2–3 hours, turning the breasts once or twice.

Line a large rimmed baking sheet with heavy-duty aluminum foil and remove the chicken from the refrigerator about 20 minutes before roasting. Preheat the oven to 500°F (260°C).

Bring a saucepan three-fourths full of water to a boil over high heat. Add the potatoes and cook until almost tender, 7–10 minutes. Using a slotted spoon, transfer the potatoes to a colander. Add the carrots to the boiling water and cook until almost tender, about 5 minutes. Transfer the carrots to the colander. In a large bowl, toss the mushrooms, red bell pepper, garlic, potatoes, and carrots with 3 tablespoons of the oil. Season with salt and pepper, and toss to coat. Add the thyme sprigs. Pour the vegetables onto the prepared baking sheet, spreading them out in a single layer. Roast for 10 minutes.

Meanwhile, in a large frying pan over medium-high heat, warm the remaining 2 tablespoons oil. Pat the chicken dry with paper towels and discard the marinade. Cook the chicken breasts skin side down until browned, 3–4 minutes. Turn the chicken and cook for another minute. Remove the baking sheet from the oven, pushing the vegetables to one side, and arrange the chicken breasts in the empty half. Roast until an instant-read thermometer inserted into the thickest part of a breast registers 170°F (77°C), 12–14 minutes.

Meanwhile, deglaze the frying pan: Pour out and discard all but 1 tablespoon of the fat, add the stock and wine, and cook over high until slightly reduced, 3–4 minutes. Season to taste with salt and pepper.

Place the chicken breasts on warmed individual plates and spoon a little sauce over each breast. Serve right away with the roasted vegetables alongside.

CHICKEN BREASTS WITH VEGETABLES & WHITE WINE

4 bone-in, skin-on chicken breast halves, about 10 oz (315 g) each

½ cup (4 fl oz/125 ml) extra-virgin olive oil

Zest of 1 lemon, grated

2 tablespoons fresh lemon juice

¼ teaspoon red pepper flakes

Kosher salt and freshly ground pepper

1 lb (500 g) Yukon gold potatoes, diced

¾ lb (375 g) carrots, peeled and thickly sliced

½ lb (250 g) fresh cremini mushrooms, brushed clean and stemmed

1 large red bell pepper, seeded and diced

2 large cloves garlic, minced

3 fresh thyme sprigs

½ cup (4 fl oz/125 ml) chicken stock or low-sodium broth

½ cup (4 fl oz/125 ml) dry white wine, or as needed

SERVES 4

Here, a savory mushroom, herb, and ricotta mixture is inserted under the skin of chicken breasts to give new life to the dinner mainstay.

MUSHROOM & RICOTTA–STUFFED CHICKEN BREASTS

FOR THE STUFFING

1 tablespoon olive oil

1 large shallot, minced

2 cremini mushrooms, brushed clean and chopped

½ cup (4 oz/125 g) whole-milk ricotta cheese

2 tablespoons minced fresh flat-leaf parsley

1 tablespoon chopped fresh chives

1 teaspoon chopped fresh tarragon

Freshly grated nutmeg

Kosher salt and freshly ground pepper

6 boneless, skin-on chicken breast halves, 6–7 oz (185–220 g) each

1 teaspoon olive oil

Kosher salt and freshly ground pepper

½ cup (4 fl oz/125 ml) dry white wine

SERVES 6

To make the stuffing, in a small sauté pan over medium heat, warm the olive oil. Add the shallot and sauté until they begin to soften, 1–2 minutes. Add the mushrooms and continue to sauté, stirring occasionally, until the mushrooms are tender, about 4 minutes. Let cool.

Meanwhile, in a bowl, stir together the cheese, parsley, chives, tarragon, and a pinch of nutmeg. Stir in the cooled mushroom mixture, and season to taste with salt and pepper.

Preheat the oven to 425°F (220°C).

Pat the chicken breasts dry with paper towels. Carefully slide your fingers under the skin on each breast, separating it from the meat but leaving it attached on one side. Spoon about 2 tablespoons stuffing directly onto the meat, spreading evenly, and pull the skin back in place to cover the filling. Flatten the filling evenly by gently pressing on the skin. Arrange the stuffed breasts skin side up in a roasting pan large enough to hold them in a single layer. Brush with 1 teaspoon oil, and sprinkle with salt and pepper.

Roast for 15 minutes. Reduce the oven temperature to 375°F (190°C). Continue to roast, basting every 10 minutes with the pan juices, until the skin is browned and an instant-read thermometer inserted into the thickest part of a breast registers 170°F (77°C), about 30 minutes.

Transfer the chicken to a plate and keep warm. Place the roasting pan on the stove top over high heat. Add the wine and deglaze the pan, stirring to remove any browned bits from the bottom of the pan. Bring to a boil and cook until reduced by half, about 5 minutes. Using a spoon, skim and discard the fat from the pan juices, then strain the juices through a fine-mesh sieve into a warmed small pitcher.

Arrange each chicken breast on a warmed individual plate and serve right away. Pass the pan juices at the table.

Starting a dish on the stove top and then finishing in the oven is ideal for the dark meat of chicken legs. Parsley, tarragon, shallot, and white wine combine to create this bright-tasting pan sauce.

In a large nonreactive bowl, stir together the lemon juice and thyme with 2 tablespoons oil, and ½ teaspoon salt. Add the chicken, turn to coat, cover, and let stand at room temperature for 1 hour.

Preheat the oven to 375°F (190°C). Pat the chicken dry with paper towels and discard the marinade.

In a large, heavy ovenproof frying pan over high heat, warm the remaining 2 tablespoons olive oil. Add the chicken skin side down and sear for about 5 minutes on the each side, reducing the heat if necessary to prevent scorching. Pour ⅓ cup (3 fl oz/ 80 ml) of the stock into the pan, and bring to a boil. Transfer the pan to the oven and roast until an instant-read thermometer inserted into the thickest part of the meat away from the bone registers 170°F (77°C), and the juices run clear when the meat is pierced at its thickest point with a knife, 40–45 minutes. Remove the pan from oven, transfer the chicken to a warmed serving platter, and let rest for 5 minutes.

Pour out and discard all but about 1 tablespoon of the fat in the pan. Place the pan on the stove top over medium-high heat, add the shallots, and sauté until softened, about 1 minute. Add the parsley and tarragon and cook for 30 seconds. Add the vermouth and stir to scrape up the browned bits on the bottom of the pan. Cook until the liquid has almost evaporated. Pour in the remaining ⅔ cup (5 fl oz/170 ml) broth and cook until slightly reduced, about 2 minutes. Whisk in the butter. Remove from the heat, season to taste with salt and pepper, and spoon the sauce over the chicken. Serve right away.

PAN-ROASTED CHICKEN LEGS WITH HERBED PAN SAUCE

¼ cup (2 fl oz/60 ml) fresh lemon juice

½ teaspoon dried thyme

¼ cup (2 fl oz/60 ml) extra-virgin olive oil

Kosher salt and freshly ground pepper

4 whole bone-in chicken legs (leg-thigh portions)

1 cup (8 fl oz/250 ml) chicken stock or low-sodium broth

2 tablespoons minced shallots

3 tablespoons chopped fresh flat-leaf parsley

1 tablespoon chopped fresh tarragon

½ cup (4 fl oz/125 ml) dry vermouth or dry white wine

1 tablespoon unsalted butter

SERVES 4–6

A conventional oven preheated to its highest setting mimics the intense heat of the traditional Indian clay-lined tandoor oven. A marinade made from yogurt and spices reinforces the Indian theme of this flavor-packed dish.

TANDOORI-STYLE CHICKEN LEGS

8 bone-in, skin-on chicken legs

Kosher salt

Juice of 1 lemon

FOR THE MARINADE

1 cup (8 oz/250 g) plain whole-milk yogurt

⅓ cup (1½ oz/45 g) chopped yellow onion

8 large fresh mint leaves, thinly sliced

1–2 serrano chiles, thinly sliced

1 tablespoon grated and peeled fresh ginger

1 large clove garlic, thinly sliced

1 teaspoon ground cumin

1 teaspoon ground coriander

1 teaspoon sweet paprika

1 teaspoon garam masala

½ teaspoon ground turmeric

Freshly ground pepper

2 tablespoons unsalted butter, melted

2 tablespoons fresh lemon juice

SERVES 6–8

Using your fingers or a small knife, remove and discard the chicken skin. Pat the chicken legs dry with paper towels. Using a sharp knife, cut through to the bone around the bottom of the drumstick about ¾ inch (2 cm) from the end. Using the knife, scrape the skin off below the cut. In each thigh, cut 3 vertical slashes, cutting through to the bone, including 1 slash through the meatiest portion of each drumstick. Season the chicken with 1 teaspoon salt, rubbing some of the salt into the slashes with your fingers. Sprinkle with the lemon juice, rubbing some into the slashes.

To make the marinade, in a blender or food processor, purée the yogurt, onion, mint, chiles, ginger, garlic, cumin, coriander, paprika, garam masala, turmeric, and ¼ teaspoon pepper.

In a shallow, glass bowl, pour the marinade over the chicken, and turn to coat. Cover and refrigerate for 12–24 hours, turning the chicken occasionally.

Remove the chicken from the refrigerator about 30 minutes before roasting. Preheat the oven to 500°F (260°C). Line a rimmed baking sheet with heavy-duty aluminum foil. Oil a flat roasting rack and place it in the prepared pan. Pat the chicken legs dry with paper towels and arrange them on the rack so they don't touch. Discard the marinade.

Roast the chicken legs until an instant-read thermometer inserted into the thickest part of the thigh away from the bone registers 170°F (77°C) and the juices run clear when the meat is pierced at its thickest point with a knife, about 25 minutes.

Meanwhile, in a small bowl, stir together the butter and lemon juice. When the chicken is ready, remove it from the oven and immediately baste it with the mixture. Transfer the chicken to a warmed serving platter and serve right away hot, warm, or at room temperature.

Here, fresh sweet cherries, a summer favorite, are lightly cooked to make a chunky compote flavored with thyme and enriched with the chicken's pan juices. The compote's lively taste balances the rich roasted chicken thighs.

CHICKEN THIGHS WITH CHERRY COMPOTE

Preheat the oven to 425°F (220°C). Lightly oil a large roasting pan. In a small bowl, stir 2 teaspoons of the thyme with 1½ teaspoons salt and ½ teaspoon pepper. Brush the chicken thighs with 2 tablespoons oil, and rub all over with the thyme mixture. Arrange the thighs, skin side up, in the prepared pan.

Roast the chicken until the skin is browned and an instant-read thermometer inserted into the thickest part of the thigh away from the bone registers 170°F (77°C) and the juices run clear when the meat is pierced at its thickest point with a knife, about 35 minutes. Transfer the chicken to a warmed serving platter.

Pour out and discard all but 1 tablespoon of the fat from the pan. Place the pan on the stove top over medium-low heat, add the shallot, and cook, scraping up the browned bits on the bottom of the pan, until softened, about 1 minute. Add the cherries and cook, stirring often, until the cherries begin to give off their juices, about 2 minutes. Add the vinegar, sugar, and the remaining 1 teaspoon thyme and stir to dissolve the sugar. Remove from the heat and season to taste with salt and pepper. Transfer the compote to a serving bowl.

Serve the chicken right away. Pass the compote at the table.

2 tablespoons extra-virgin olive oil, plus more for greasing

3 teaspoons minced fresh thyme

Kosher salt and freshly ground pepper

8 bone-in, skin-on chicken thighs, about 3 lb (1.5 kg) total weight

1 small shallot, minced

1 lb (500 g) fresh bing cherries, pitted and coarsely chopped

2 tablespoons balsamic vinegar

2 tablespoons firmly packed golden brown sugar

SERVES 4

For this crisp-skinned bird, a mixture of chopped fresh herbs is rubbed under the skin before roasting. We've included instructions for trussing the chicken, which helps it to cook evenly and create a uniform shape, but you can skip that step if you like.

HERB & GARLIC CHICKEN

1 whole chicken, about
4–5 lb (2–2.5 kg)

4 teaspoons chopped fresh
rosemary, plus 1 sprig

2 tablespoons chopped
fresh thyme, plus 3 sprigs

4 teaspoons chopped fresh
sage, plus 2 sprigs

¼ cup (2 oz/60 ml)
extra-virgin olive oil,
plus more for coating

Kosher salt and freshly
ground pepper

½ small yellow onion

3 large cloves garlic

SERVES 4–6

Preheat the oven to 425°F (220°C). If the giblets are in the chicken cavity, remove them and reserve for another use or discard. Remove and discard any excess fat on the chicken.

In a small bowl, stir together half each of the chopped rosemary, thyme, and sage, along with ¼ cup (2 oz/60 ml) oil. Season to taste with pepper.

Starting from the neck end, gently separate the skin from the meat using your fingers, being careful not to tear the skin. Rotate the bird 180 degrees, and loosen the skin above the cavity the same way, reaching in as far as possible to loosen the skin on the tops of the thighs and legs.

Slide the herb mixture under the skin, and rub it evenly over the exposed meat, covering it as much as possible. Pat the skin back into place, and tuck the wing tips under the shoulders.

Season the cavity with 2 teaspoons salt, and then stuff with the herb sprigs, onion, and garlic, pushing them in as far as they will go. Tie the legs together with kitchen string. (The chicken can be prepared up to this point a day in advance, wrapped well, and refrigerated.)

Rub the bird all over with oil and sprinkle generously with salt and the remaining chopped herbs. In a roasting pan, roast the chicken breast side up until the skin is browned and an instant-read thermometer inserted in the thickest part of the thigh away from the bone registers 170°F (77°C), about 1 hour and 10 minutes (12–15 minutes per lb/500 g). Transfer the chicken to a carving board and let rest for 15 minutes.

Carve the chicken and arrange on a warmed serving platter. Serve right away.

Chicken roasts quickly when butterflied, delivering wonderfully crisp skin and succulent meat in only about 45 minutes.

CRISP-SKINNED BUTTERFLIED CHICKEN

1 small chicken, about 2½–3 lb (1.25–1.5 kg)

FOR THE MARINADE

¼ cup (2 fl oz/60 ml) dry white wine

2 green onions, including tender green tops, thickly sliced

2 tablespoons extra-virgin olive oil

2 cloves garlic, smashed

1 teaspoon fresh thyme leaves

Kosher salt and freshly ground pepper

SERVES 2

If the giblets and neck are in the chicken cavity, remove them and reserve for another use or discard. Remove and discard any excess fat on the chicken. Butterfly the chicken (see page 81). Pat the chicken dry with paper towels and place the bird in a nonreactive dish.

To make the marinade, in a blender or food processor, purée the wine, green onions, oil, garlic, thyme, and ½ teaspoon each salt and pepper. Pour the marinade on top of the chicken, and turn to coat. Cover and refrigerate for 3–4 hours, turning the chicken once or twice.

Remove the chicken from the refrigerator about 30 minutes before roasting. Preheat the oven to 450°F (230°C).

Select a roasting pan large enough to hold the chicken comfortably and line it with heavy-duty aluminum foil. Oil a flat roasting rack and place it in the prepared pan. Pat the chicken dry with paper towels and arrange it skin side up on the rack. Discard the marinade.

Roast until the skin is browned and until an instant-read thermometer inserted into the thickest part of a thigh away from the bone registers 170°F (77°C), 40–45 minutes. Transfer the chicken to a carving board and let rest for 10 minutes. Cut the chicken in half by cutting along each side of the breastbone with a sharp knife or poultry shears. Transfer to a warmed serving platter and serve right away.

Distinctively earthy and intensely fragrant, black truffles season this crisp chicken. An infused pan sauce finishes this indulgent dish.

CRISP CHICKEN WITH TRUFFLE BUTTER

1 whole chicken, about 4 lb (2 kg)

Grapeseed oil, for greasing

6 tablespoons (3 oz/90 g) truffle butter, at room temperature

Kosher salt and freshly ground pepper

1 small onion, diced

1 small carrot, thickly sliced

1 small celery stalk, thickly sliced

1 cup (8 fl oz/250 ml) chicken stock or low-sodium broth

SERVES 4

If present, remove the giblets and reserve for another use or discard. Remove any excess fat from the chicken and coarsely chop the fat. In a small saucepan over low heat, cook the fat until rendered, about 15 minutes. Strain through a fine-mesh sieve; you should have about 1½ tablespoons fat. Let the chicken and fat stand at room temperature for 1–2 hours.

Preheat the oven to 425°F (220°C). Oil a V-shaped roasting rack in a roasting pan.

Starting from the neck end, gently separate the skin from the meat with your fingers, being careful not to tear the skin. Rotate the bird 180 degrees, and loosen the skin above the cavity the same way, reaching in to loosen the skin on the tops of the thighs and legs. Slip about 4 tablespoons (2 oz/60 g) of the truffle butter under the skin and rub the chicken to distribute the butter evenly. Rub the rendered fat all over the exterior of the chicken and sprinkle the chicken inside and out with 2 teaspoons salt and ½ teaspoon pepper. Place the chicken on its side on the prepared rack in the pan. Roast for 20 minutes, then turn the chicken on its other side and roast for 20 minutes longer. Turn the chicken onto its back and add the onion, carrot, and celery to the pan. Continue to roast the chicken until browned and an instant-read thermometer inserted into the thickest part of the breast registers 170°F (77°C), 30–40 minutes. Tilt the chicken so any juice in the cavity flows into the pan. Transfer the chicken to a carving board and let rest for 10 minutes.

Remove and discard the vegetables in the pan. Pour the pan juices into a glass measuring cup, let stand for about 2 minutes, then use a spoon to skim off the surface fat. Return the pan juices to the roasting pan and place the pan on the stove top over medium heat. Add the stock and bring to a boil, scraping up the browned bits from the bottom of the pan. Remove from the heat and whisk in the remaining truffle butter, 1 tablespoon at a time. Season with salt and pepper.

Carve the chicken and arrange on warmed dinner plates. Pour some of the sauce over each serving and serve right away.

Butterflying the bird allows it to cook faster while keeping it juicy. This particular preparation is flavored simply, adopting an Italian flair with fennel seeds, garlic, and lemon.

BUTTERFLIED CHICKEN WITH LEMONS

Preheat the oven to 450°F (230°C).

If the giblets are in the chicken cavity, remove them and reserve for another use or discard. Remove and discard any excess fat on the chicken. Lay the chicken skin side up in a roasting pan large enough to hold it comfortably. In a small bowl, whisk together the olive oil and fennel seeds. Rub the chicken all over with the fennel oil. Squeeze 1 lemon half over the chicken and sprinkle with 1 teaspoon salt and several grinds of pepper. Cut the remaining lemon half into small chunks and strew them over and around the chicken along with the garlic cloves.

Roast the chicken for 20 minutes. Reduce the heat to 400°F (200°C) and roast until the skin is browned and an instant-read thermometer inserted into the thickest part of the thigh away from the bone registers 170°F (77°C), about 40 minutes longer. Transfer to a carving board and let rest for 10 minutes.

To serve, using clean poultry shears or a chef's knife, cut the chicken into 10 serving pieces (2 legs, 2 thighs, 2 wings, and 4 breast pieces). Transfer to a warmed serving platter and spoon the pan juices, including the garlic and lemon pieces, over the chicken. Serve right away.

1 whole chicken, about 4 lb (2 kg), butterflied (see page 81)

¼ cup (2 fl oz/60 ml) extra-virgin olive oil

1 teaspoon crushed fennel seeds

1 lemon, halved

Kosher salt and freshly ground pepper

8 cloves garlic

SERVES 4

This lively take on roast chicken features a bold, Latin-style spice blend rubbed all over the skin. Serve with black beans and white rice.

CHILE-LIME CHICKEN

1 whole chicken, about
3–3½ lb (1.5–1.75 kg)

FOR THE SPICE RUB

2 tablespoons sweet paprika

1 serrano chile, seeded
and minced

2 cloves garlic, crushed

1 teaspoon chili powder

½ teaspoon dried thyme

¾ cup (6 fl oz/180 ml)
chicken stock or
low-sodium broth

Kosher salt and freshly
ground pepper

½ cup (¾ oz/20 g) chopped
fresh cilantro

2 limes, cut into wedges

SERVES 4

If the giblets are in the chicken cavity, remove them and reserve for another use or discard. Remove and discard any excess fat from the chicken. Preheat the oven to 400°F (200°C).

To make the spice rub, stir together the paprika, chile, garlic, chili powder, and thyme in a small bowl.

Pat the chicken dry with paper towels and place the chicken breast side up in an oiled heavy roasting pan large enough to hold it comfortably. Rub the spice rub all over the chicken. Roast until the skin is browned and an instant-read thermometer inserted into the thickest part of the thigh away from the bone registers 170°F (77°C), about 50–60 minutes. Transfer the chicken to a carving board and let rest for 10 minutes.

Meanwhile, place the roasting pan on the stove top over medium-high heat, and, using a spoon, skim off the surface fat. Add the stock and cook, scraping up the browned bits on the bottom of the pan. Bring the liquid to a boil and cook until reduced by half, about 4 minutes. Season to taste with salt and pepper.

Carve the chicken and arrange on a warmed serving platter. Sprinkle with the cilantro. Drizzle the pan sauce over the chicken and serve right away, accompanied by the lime wedges for squeezing.

Filled with a savory bread stuffing, this chicken tastes just like a Thanksgiving-style bird, but is perfect for an easy Sunday supper for a crowd.

CHICKEN WITH HERBED BREAD STUFFING

To make the stuffing, preheat the oven to 350°F (180°C). Arrange the bread cubes in a single layer on a baking sheet. Bake, turning twice, until golden, about 15 minutes. Set aside. In a large frying pan over medium heat, melt the butter. Add the onion and sauté until translucent, about 5 minutes. In a large bowl, toss the bread cubes, onion, parsley, and sage. Season to taste with salt and pepper. Set aside.

Raise the oven temperature to 400°F (200°C).

If the giblets are in the chicken cavity, remove them and reserve for another use or discard. Remove and discard any excess fat on the chicken. Pat the chicken dry with paper towels. Starting from the neck end, gently separate the skin from the meat over the breast using your fingers, being careful not to tear the skin. Rotate the bird 180 degrees and loosen the skin above the cavity the same way, reaching in as far as possible to loosen the skin on the tops of the thighs and legs. Slide the sage leaves under the skin and sprinkle inside and out with salt and pepper. Fill the chicken with the stuffing, and tie the legs together with kitchen string. Brush the chicken with the melted butter and place the chicken, breast side up, in an oiled roasting pan, and add the onion.

Roast the chicken until the skin is browned and an instant-read thermometer inserted into the thickest part of the thigh registers 170°F (77°C), 1–1¼ hours.

Transfer the chicken to a carving board and let rest for 10 minutes. Meanwhile, place the pan on the stove top over medium-high heat and, using a spoon, skim off the surface fat. Add the stock and bring to a boil, scraping up the browned bits in the bottom of the pan. Cook until reduced by half, about 4 minutes. In a food processor or blender, purée the pan sauce and onion. Season to taste with salt and pepper.

Carve the chicken and arrange on a warmed platter. Pour the sauce on top and serve right away with the stuffing alongside.

FOR THE HERB STUFFING

2–2½ cups (4–5 oz/125–155 g) trimmed white bread cubes

¼ cup (2 oz/60 g) unsalted butter

1 yellow onion, chopped

½ cup (¾ oz/20 g) finely chopped fresh flat-leaf parsley

2 teaspoons finely chopped fresh sage or 1 teaspoon dried

Kosher salt and freshly ground pepper

1 whole chicken, about 4½–5½ lb (2.25–2.75 kg)

5 fresh sage leaves

Kosher salt and freshly ground pepper

2 tablespoons unsalted butter, melted

1 large yellow onion, sliced

¾ cup (6 fl oz/180 ml) chicken stock or low-sodium broth

SERVES 5–6

Soaking a turkey in a salt-and-sugar brine adds moisture to the meat. It is an especially useful technique for all-white meat, which can become dry with roasting. Be mindful when seasoning the pan gravy, as the brine will already contribute some saltiness to the dish. You'll need to plan ahead for this recipe: The turkey must be put into the brine 28 hours before cooking.

TURKEY BREASTS WITH LEMON-PARSLEY GRAVY

FOR THE BRINE

6 qt (6 l) water

2 cups (16 oz/500 g) kosher salt

1½ cups (10½ oz/330 g) firmly packed golden brown sugar

2 whole bone-in turkey breasts, about 11 lbs (5.5 kg) total weight

9 tablespoons (4½ oz/ 140 g) unsalted butter, at room temperature

1 yellow onion, unpeeled and quartered

2 large carrots, unpeeled and coarsely chopped

1¾ cups (14 fl oz/430 ml) chicken stock or low-sodium broth

continued

To make the brine, combine the water, salt, and brown sugar in a stockpot. Cook, stirring, over medium heat just until the salt and sugar dissolve. Let cool to room temperature.

Pat the turkey dry with paper towels. In 1 very large or 2 large nonreactive bowls, cover the turkey breasts with the brine. Refrigerate for 24 hours, turning the breasts occasionally in the brine. Drain and discard the brine. Cover the turkey breasts with fresh, cold water and let stand at room temperature, turning once or twice, for 4 hours. Drain and pat dry with paper towels. Remove and discard any excess skin from the turkey breasts.

Position a rack in the lower third of the oven and preheat to 325°F (165°C). Spread 1½ tablespoons of the butter over each turkey breast. Place the breasts on a rack in a roasting pan. Scatter the onion and carrots in the pan around the turkey. Roast for 30 minutes.

Meanwhile, in a small saucepan, heat the chicken stock with the white wine, oil, lemon juice, and the remaining butter over low heat until the butter has melted. At the 30-minute mark, baste the breasts with some of the broth mixture.

Continue to roast the turkey, basting every 30 minutes with the remaining broth mixture and then with the accumulated pan juices, and stirring the vegetables in the pan occasionally, until the breasts are browned and an instant-read thermometer inserted into the thickest part of a breast registers 170°F (77°C), about 2 hours total roasting time.

Transfer the breasts to a carving board and let rest for 5 minutes.

To make the gravy, heat the roasting pan with the vegetables and juices on the stove top over medium-high heat. Add 6¾ cups (54 fl oz/1.7 l) of the chicken stock to the pan and bring to a brisk simmer. Stir to deglaze the pan, scraping up the browned bits from the bottom of the pan, about 5 minutes. Pour the contents of the pan through a sieve set over a large bowl, pressing hard on the vegetables with the back of a large spoon to extract all the liquid; discard the solids. Using a spoon, skim and discard as much of the surface fat as possible. Transfer the remaining liquid to a wide saucepan. Cook over medium-high heat until reduced by one-fourth, about 10 minutes.

In a small bowl, stir the remaining ¼ cup (2 fl oz/60 ml) chicken stock into the cornstarch to make a slurry. Gradually stir the slurry into the simmering gravy. Stir in the parsley, lemon juice, and the lemon zest. Cook until the gravy clears and thickens, about 1 minute. Season to taste with salt and pepper. Carve the turkey by slicing it against the grain on a diagonal. Serve right away with the gravy.

½ cup (4 fl oz/125 ml) dry white wine

¼ cup (2 fl oz/60 ml) peanut or canola oil

1 tablespoon fresh lemon juice

FOR THE GRAVY

7 cups (56 fl oz/1.75 l) chicken stock or low-sodium broth

¼ cup (1 oz/30 g) cornstarch

⅓ cup (½ oz/15 g) minced fresh flat-leaf parsley

1 tablespoon fresh lemon juice

1 tablespoon minced lemon zest

Kosher salt and freshly ground pepper

SERVES 8–10

In this innovative recipe, a paste made from olives, shallots, and herbs is rubbed underneath the skin of the turkey breast, penetrating the meat and imbuing it with the flavors of Southern France. Use the sliced leftover turkey for sandwiches the next day.

TURKEY BREAST WITH PROVENÇAL FLAVORS

1 carrot, peeled and chopped

1 celery stalk, chopped

2 small yellow onions, chopped

1 whole bone-in, skin-on turkey breast, 5–6 lb (2.5–3 kg)

1 lemon, halved

Kosher salt and freshly ground pepper

FOR THE SEASONING PASTE

1 generous cup (6 oz/185 g) pitted oil-cured black olives

½ cup (½ oz/15 g) firmly packed fresh flat-leaf parsley leaves

4 shallots

1 tablespoon herbes de Provence

½ teaspoon freshly ground pepper

1 tablespoon olive oil

SERVES 8–10

Preheat the oven to 400°F (200°C).

Scatter the chopped carrot, celery, and half the onions in the bottom of a large roasting pan. Set a rack over the vegetables. Pat the turkey dry with paper towels. Rub the inside with the lemon, and sprinkle with salt and pepper.

To make the seasoning paste, in a food processor, combine the olives, parsley, shallots, herbes de Provence, and pepper, pulsing until evenly chopped but not smooth.

Gently separate the skin from the meat over the breast using your fingers, leaving the skin attached on the sides. Spread the seasoning paste under the skin, in the wing sockets, and inside the cavity. Fill the cavity with the remaining chopped onion. Brush the skin with the oil and set the turkey breast, on one side, on the rack.

Roast until the skin is browned, 15–20 minutes. Turn the breast on the opposite side and continue to roast until the skin on the second side is browned, 15–20 minutes. Reduce the oven temperature to 350°F (180°C), turn the breast side up and continue to roast, basting every 10 minutes with the pan juices during the last 30 minutes, until the skin is browned and an instant-read thermometer registers 170°F (77°C), about 2 hours longer. If the turkey skin is browning too quickly, tent with aluminum foil.

Transfer the turkey breast to a carving board and let rest for 15 minutes. Cut the turkey across the grain into thin slices. Arrange them on a warmed platter, along with the vegetables from the roasting pan, if desired, and serve right away.

Fresh sage is a classic flavoring for Thanksgiving turkey, and it's used liberally here, in both the rub that coats the outside of the bird as well as the stuffing that is cooked along with it. It's important to cool the stuffing completely before placing it in the cavity of the bird to ensure proper cooking.

SAGE-RUBBED TURKEY

FOR THE SAGE RUB

2 tablespoons chopped fresh sage

4 cloves garlic, chopped

Grated zest of 1 lemon

1 teaspoon ground sage

Kosher salt and freshly ground pepper

1 turkey, about 12 lb (6 kg)

FOR THE STUFFING

1 loaf (1 lb/500 g) sourdough bread, diced

2 tablespoons unsalted butter

1 lb (500 g) sweet Italian sausage, casings removed

1 yellow onion, chopped

1 leek, including tender green tops, chopped

1 celery stalk, chopped

¼ cup (⅓ oz/10 g) chopped fresh sage

1 cup (8 fl oz/250 ml) half-and-half

½ cup (¾ oz/20 g) chopped fresh flat-leaf parsley

1½ cups (12 fl oz/375 ml) chicken stock or low-sodium broth

continued

To make the sage rub, in a spice grinder, combine the chopped sage, garlic, lemon zest, and ground sage with 2 tablespoons salt and 2 teaspoons pepper until finely ground.

If the giblets and neck are in the turkey cavity, reserve for another use or discard. Remove and discard any excess fat from the cavity. Rub the sage mixture all over the skin and inside both cavities of the turkey. Place the bird on a baking sheet, cover tightly with plastic wrap, and refrigerate for 24 hours.

To make the stuffing, preheat the oven to 350°F (180°C). Spread the bread cubes on a rimmed baking sheet and toast in the oven until golden, about 20 minutes. Remove from the oven and set aside to cool.

In a large frying pan over medium heat, melt the butter. Add the sausage, onion, leek, celery, and sage and cook, breaking up the meat with a wooden spoon, until the meat browns and is cooked through and the vegetables are translucent, about 10 minutes. Remove from the heat and fold in the bread cubes, half-and-half, and parsley. Stir in the stock until the mixture is evenly moistened. Season to taste with salt and pepper. Let cool completely before stuffing into the turkey cavity.

Remove the turkey from the refrigerator about 1 hour before roasting. Position a rack in the lower third of the oven and preheat to 425°F (220°C). Pat the turkey dry with paper towels. Spoon the stuffing into the neck and body cavities, packing it loosely. Cross the drumsticks and, using kitchen string, tie the legs together. Tuck the wings underneath the body. Arrange the carrot, celery, and onion in a large, heavy roasting pan and add the wine. Place the bird, breast side up, on the vegetables.

Roast the turkey for 45 minutes. Reduce the heat to 350°F (180°C) and continue roasting, basting with the pan juices every 30 minutes, until an instant-read thermometer inserted into the thickest part of the thigh away from the bone registers 170°F (77°C), 2½–3 hours. Transfer the turkey to a carving board and let rest for 15–20 minutes.

Meanwhile, in a small saucepan, heat the broth over medium until simmering. Pour the juices from the roasting pan into a heatproof measuring pitcher. Using a spoon, skim off 3 tablespoons of the fat and return it to the roasting pan. Skim off and discard the remaining fat from the measuring pitcher and pour the remaining juices into the simmering broth. Place the roasting pan on the stove top over medium heat. Sprinkle in the flour while stirring continuously with a wooden spoon, scraping up any brown bits on the bottom of the pan. Stream in the hot broth while whisking constantly to break up any lumps that form. Reduce the heat to low and simmer, stirring occasionally to prevent scorching, until slightly thickened, about 5 minutes. Season to taste with salt and pepper. Pour the gravy through a fine-mesh sieve into a warmed bowl for passing at the table.

Remove the string and scoop the stuffing out of the turkey into a warmed large bowl. Carve the turkey and arrange the pieces on a warmed serving platter. Serve right away.

Kosher salt and freshly ground pepper

1 carrot, peeled and chopped

1 celery stalk, chopped

1 yellow onion, chopped

2 cups (16 fl oz/500 ml) dry white wine

2 cups (16 fl oz/500 ml) chicken stock or low-sodium broth

3 tablespoons all-purpose flour

Kosher salt and freshly ground pepper

SERVES 8–10

Brining is the answer to the perennial question of how to roast a turkey long enough to cook the dark meat through without overcooking the white meat. If you do not have a pot large enough to hold the turkey in brine, use a large ice chest and add a small bag of ice to the brine.

If the giblets are in the turkey cavity, reserve for another use or discard. Remove and discard any excess fat from the cavity. Choose a stockpot large enough to hold the turkey and fit inside your refrigerator. Fill the pot one-third full with cold water. Stir in the 3 cups (1½ lb/750 g) salt, the sugar, onion, thyme, and peppercorns. Add the turkey breast side down, and fill with as much water as possible. Cover and refrigerate for 24 hours.

Two hours before roasting, rinse the turkey inside and out under cold running water and discard the brine. Return the turkey to the pot and add cold water to cover. Let stand at room temperature to remove additional brine from the bird.

To roast the turkey, position a rack in the lower third of the oven and preheat to 325°F (165°C). Drain the turkey and pat dry with paper towels inside and out. Gently separate the skin from the meat over the breast using your fingers, carefully leaving it attached on the sides. Spread half of the softened butter under the skin over the breast, then insert about 12 large sage leaves under the skin, spacing them evenly apart. Sprinkle the neck and body cavities with pepper (do not salt, as the bird was brined) and place the remaining sage sprigs in the body cavity. Truss the turkey, if desired. Turn the bird on its back and rub all over with the remaining softened butter. Place the bird breast side up on a rack in a large roasting pan. In a bowl, combine the melted butter and oil to use for basting.

Pour 1 inch (2.5 cm) of water into the bottom of the roasting pan and roast the turkey for 3–3½ hours, basting the turkey every hour with the butter mixture and adding water to the pan if needed. Begin testing for doneness after 2½ hours, and cook until an instant-read thermometer inserted into the thickest part of the thigh away from the bone registers 170°F (77°C). *continued*

BRINED TURKEY WITH CORN BREAD & SAUSAGE DRESSING

1 turkey, about 14 lb (7 kg)

3 cups (1½ lb/750 g) kosher salt, plus more for seasoning

½ cup (4 oz/125 g) sugar

1 small yellow onion, chopped

1 bunch fresh thyme

1 tablespoon black peppercorns, cracked

4 tablespoons (2 oz/60 g) unsalted butter, at room temperature, plus 4 tablespoons unsalted butter, melted

Freshly ground pepper

1 bunch fresh sage

½ cup (4 fl oz/125 ml) olive oil

continued

SERVES 10

FOR THE DRESSING

Prepared 8-inch (20-cm)
square loaf day-old
corn bread, crumbled

2 tablespoons
unsalted butter

2 tablespoons olive oil

3 sweet Italian sausages,
casings removed

1 small yellow onion,
finely chopped

3 celery stalks with leaves,
finely chopped

3 large eggs, beaten

2 tablespoons minced
fresh flat-leaf parsley

1 teaspoon dried thyme,
crumbled

Fine sea salt and freshly
ground pepper

About 1½ cups (12 fl oz/
375 ml) chicken or turkey
stock, or low-sodium broth

FOR THE GRAVY

⅓ cup (2 oz/60 g)
all-purpose flour

½ cup (4 fl oz/125 ml) dry
white vermouth

1½ cups (12 fl oz/375 ml)
good-quality chicken stock
or low-sodium broth, plus
additional as needed

Fine sea salt and freshly
ground pepper

Transfer the turkey to a carving board and let rest for 30 minutes. Meanwhile, make the dressing: Butter a 9-by-13-inch (23-by-33-cm) baking dish. Put the corn bread in a large bowl. In a large frying pan, melt the butter with the oil over medium heat. Add the sausages and cook, stirring occasionally, until lightly browned, about 5 minutes. Add the onion and cook until translucent, 2–3 minutes; transfer the mixture and the celery to the large bowl and toss well. Stir in the eggs, parsley, thyme, ½ teaspoon salt, and ½ teaspoon pepper. Stir in just enough of the stock as needed to make a moist mixture. Transfer to the buttered dish and cover with aluminum foil. Transfer the dressing to the oven and bake about 45 minutes before the turkey is done. Remove the foil and bake until lightly browned and crisp on top, about 20 minutes longer.

To make the gravy, pour the turkey drippings from the roasting pan into a large glass measuring pitcher. Let the fat rise to the surface, then pour or spoon off all the fat, reserving ¼ cup (2 fl oz/ 60 ml). Return the reserved fat to the pan. Place the pan over 2 burners on the stove top and heat over medium. Stir in the flour and cook, stirring constantly, for 2–3 minutes. Add the vermouth and stir to scrape up the browned bits from the bottom of the pan. Add enough stock to the drippings to make 2 cups (16 fl oz/500 ml), and cook, stirring, until the gravy thickens, about 5 minutes. Add more stock, if needed, and season to taste with salt and pepper.

Carve the turkey and serve right away, passing the gravy and dressing at the table.

Sweet and slightly smoky maple syrup balances the spiciness of mustard to make a simple glaze for lean turkey tenderloins. A splash of Port flavors a bold, sweet-sour sauce of fresh cranberries and crystallized ginger.

MAPLE-MUSTARD TURKEY TENDERLOINS WITH CRANBERRY-GINGER RELISH

Preheat the oven to 350°F (180°C).

Using kitchen string, tie each tenderloin crosswise in 3 or 4 places, spacing the ties at even intervals. Season the tenderloins with 1 teaspoon salt and ½ teaspoon pepper.

In a large ovenproof frying pan over medium-high heat, warm the oil. Add the turkey and cook until browned on all sides, about 5 minutes. Remove from the heat.

In a small bowl, stir together the maple syrup and mustard. Spread about half of the mixture over the tenderloins. Place the pan in the oven and cook for 10 minutes.

Spread the remaining maple syrup mixture over the turkey, return to the oven, and continue to cook until an instant-read thermometer inserted in the center of a tenderloin registers 170°F (77°C), about 10 minutes longer.

While the turkey is roasting, in a heavy saucepan, combine the cranberries, Port, sugar, and crystallized ginger and bring to a boil over high heat, stirring often. Reduce the heat to medium and cook, uncovered, at a brisk simmer, stirring often, until the berries have popped and the juices are syrupy, about 10 minutes. Meanwhile, fill a large bowl with ice water. When the sauce is ready, transfer it to a heatproof bowl and nest the bowl in the ice bath. Let cool, then transfer to a serving bowl.

When the tenderloins are ready, transfer them to a carving board and let rest for 5 minutes. Snip the strings and cut the tenderloins crosswise into slices ½ inch (12 mm) thick.

Divide the turkey evenly among warmed plates. Spoon some of the cranberry sauce next to each portion and serve right away. Pass the remaining sauce at the table.

2 turkey tenderloins, about 12 oz (375 g) each

Kosher salt and freshly ground pepper

1 tablespoon grapeseed oil

2 tablespoons pure maple syrup

1 tablespoon Dijon mustard

1¾ cups (7 oz/220 g) fresh cranberries

½ cup (4 fl oz/125 ml) Port

½ cup (4 oz/125 g) sugar

3 tablespoons minced crystallized ginger

SERVES 4–6

A small roast turkey makes a great main dish for company or family dinners any time of the year. Leftovers are always welcome for a quick midweek meal or for sandwiches. Here, a flavorful roasted garlic and herb butter is stuffed under the skin. The bird is turned twice during roasting to produce evenly browned and crisp skin.

TURKEY WITH ROASTED GARLIC & PARSLEY

1 large head garlic

2 tablespoons olive oil

1 turkey, about 12 lb (6 kg)

3 tablespoons unsalted butter, at room temperature

3 tablespoons chopped fresh flat-leaf parsley

1/2 teaspoon finely chopped fresh sage

Kosher salt and freshly ground pepper

continued

Preheat the oven to 300°F (150°C).

Using a small, sharp knife, score the garlic around the middle, cutting through the papery skin but not into the cloves. Remove the top half of the skin and expose the cloves. Lightly oil a small baking dish and set the garlic head in the pan. Drizzle the olive oil evenly over the top of the garlic, then sprinkle evenly with salt and pepper. Cover the dish with aluminum foil. Roast the garlic for 1 hour. Set aside to cool.

Remove the turkey from the refrigerator 1 hour before roasting. Preheat the oven to 325°F (165°C). Oil a V-shaped roasting rack and place it in a roasting pan just large enough to hold the turkey. If the giblets and neck are in the turkey cavity, reserve for another use or discard. Remove and discard any excess fat from the cavity. Pat the turkey dry with paper towels.

With the turkey breast side up, and starting at the neck cavity, gently separate the skin from the meat over the breast using your fingers. Then, starting at the body cavity, gently separate the skin from the thigh and drumstick meat. Separate the garlic cloves and squeeze the softened pulp into a small bowl. Add 2 tablespoons of the butter, the parsley, the sage, 1/2 teaspoon salt, and pepper to taste and mash together with a fork. Push this mixture under the turkey skin, distributing it evenly over the breast and legs. Cross the drumsticks and, using kitchen string, tie the legs together. Tuck the wings underneath the body. Rub the turkey all over with the remaining 1 tablespoon butter. Place the turkey on its side on the rack.

Roast the turkey for 45 minutes. Remove the pan from the oven and carefully turn the turkey on its other side. Continue to roast another 45 minutes. Remove from the oven again and turn the turkey breast side up. Continue to roast until a thermometer inserted into the thickest part of the thigh away from the bone registers 170°F (77°C), about 1 hour longer. Remove the pan from the oven, transfer the turkey to a carving board, and let rest for 15–20 minutes.

While the bird rests, make the sauce: Place the butter and flour in a small bowl and mix together with a fork to make a paste. Deglaze the roasting pan using the chicken broth and wine. Pour the contents of the pan through a medium-mesh sieve into a small saucepan, bring to a boil, and boil until reduced to about 2 cups (16 fl oz/500 ml), 5–7 minutes. Reduce the heat to low, whisk the flour-butter paste into the liquid a little at a time, and simmer until slightly thickened, 3–4 minutes. Season to taste with salt and pepper, pour into a small pitcher, and keep warm.

Carve the turkey (see page 85) and serve right away, passing the sauce at the table.

FOR THE SAUCE

2 tablespoons unsalted butter, at room temperature

2 tablespoons all-purpose flour

2 cups (16 fl oz/500 ml) chicken stock or low-sodium broth

1/2 cup (4 fl oz/125 ml) dry white wine

Kosher salt and freshly ground pepper

SERVES 8

The method of steaming the duck legs before roasting helps melt away some of the excess fat and render the skin astonishingly crisp.

_____

Pat the duck dry with paper towels. In a shallow, nonreactive bowl large enough to hold the duck legs, stir together the oil, vinegar, garlic, shallot, thyme, ½ teaspoon salt, and a few grates of pepper. Add the duck legs, turn to coat, cover, and refrigerate for 3–4 hours, turning the legs once or twice. Remove the duck legs from the marinade. Pour the marinade into a saucepan, and bring to a boil over high heat. Remove from the heat and reserve to use as a glaze.

Select a pot large enough to hold a footed flat rack on which the duck legs will stand, at least 2 inches (5 cm) above the bottom of the pot. (If you do not have a footed rack, rest a rack on 2 inverted small heatproof cups or bowls.) Add water to a depth of about 1 inch (2.5 cm). Place the duck legs skin side up on the rack. Bring the water to a boil, cover tightly, and steam the duck until the skin is translucent, about 20 minutes.

Meanwhile, preheat the oven to 450°F (230°C). Line a roasting pan large enough to hold the duck legs in a single layer with heavy-duty aluminum foil. Place a flat rack in the pan.

When the duck legs are ready, transfer them skin side up to the rack in the prepared pan. Brush the skin with some of the glaze, and roast until the skin is brown and crisp and a thermometer inserted into the thickest part of a thigh away from the bone registers 170°F (77°C), about 20 minutes. Remove the pan from the oven and brush the drumsticks again with the glaze. Tent with aluminum foil and let rest for 5 minutes.

Meanwhile, prepare the mushrooms: In a large frying pan over medium-high heat, warm the oil. Add the mushrooms and green onion and sauté until the mushrooms release their liquid, about 2 minutes. Add the vinegar and thyme and sprinkle with salt and pepper. Cook until the mushrooms are softened and most of the liquid has evaporated, 2–3 minutes longer. Transfer the duck legs to warmed individual plates and spoon the mushrooms alongside. Serve right away.

BALSAMIC DUCK LEGS WITH MUSHROOMS

4–6 bone-in, skin-on duck legs, about 6 oz (185 g) each

3 tablespoons extra-virgin olive oil

3 tablespoons balsamic vinegar

2 cloves garlic, thinly sliced

1 small shallot, thinly sliced

3 or 4 fresh thyme sprigs, lightly bruised

Kosher salt and freshly ground pepper

FOR THE MUSHROOMS

2 tablespoons extra-virgin olive oil

½ lb (250 g) fresh cremini mushrooms, brushed clean, stems removed, and caps thickly sliced

1 green onion, including tender green parts, thinly sliced

2 tablespoons balsamic vinegar

½ teaspoon fresh thyme leaves

Kosher salt and freshly ground pepper

SERVES 4

Duck's rich meat is complemented by tangy fruits like oranges and cherries and bold spices, such as Chinese five-spice powder. Think of this dish for a special-occasion meal—your guests will be impressed by the well-browned, crisp duck skin and succulent meat, but they won't realize how easy it was to achieve those results using a pan-roasting technique. Serve the same wine at the table that you use for the sauce, ideally a fruity Pinot Noir, which has a great affinity for both duck and the dried cherries used in the sauce.

PAN-ROASTED DUCK BREASTS WITH DRIED-CHERRY SAUCE

FOR THE SPICE RUB

1 teaspoon sweet paprika

1 teaspoon ground coriander

1 teaspoon Chinese five-spice powder

Kosher salt and freshly ground pepper

4 boneless, skin-on duck breasts, 5–6 oz (165–185 g) each

2 teaspoons extra-virgin olive oil

FOR THE SAUCE

1 cup (8 fl oz/250 ml) hearty red wine

1 cup (8 fl oz/250 ml) chicken stock or low-sodium broth

continued

To make the spice rub, in a small bowl, stir together the paprika, coriander, five-spice powder, 1/2 teaspoon salt, and several grinds of pepper.

Using a small, sharp knife, score the skin of the duck breasts in a crisscross diamond pattern, being careful not to cut into the flesh. Brush the duck breasts with the oil and sprinkle the rub on both sides of each breast. Let the duck breasts stand at room temperature for 30 minutes.

Preheat the oven to 450°F (230°C).

To make the sauce, in a saucepan, combine the wine, stock, orange zest, orange juice, shallots, and peppercorns and bring to a boil over high heat. Reduce the heat to medium-high and cook until reduced by half, about 10 minutes. Strain the mixture through a medium-mesh sieve into a bowl; discard the contents of the sieve. Return the strained liquid to the pan. Add the cherries and honey, and bring to a simmer over medium heat. Simmer until the cherries are plumped, 4–5 minutes. Whisk in the butter. Dissolve the cornstarch in1 tablespoon water. Gradually whisk in the cornstarch mixture and cook, stirring, until the sauce thickens, about 2 minutes. Adjust the seasonings and keep warm.

Heat a large cast-iron or heavy ovenproof frying pan over high heat until very hot. Place the breasts, skin side down, in the pan and sear until the skin is nicely browned, 3–4 minutes. Turn the breasts over and cook for 1 minute longer. Spoon the fat from the bottom of the pan and discard. Transfer the pan to the oven and roast the duck until an instant-read thermometer inserted into the thickest part of a breast registers 130°–135°F (54°–57°C) for medium-rare, about 8 minutes, or until done to your liking. Remove from the oven, transfer the breasts to a carving board, and tent with aluminum foil. Let the duck breasts rest for 3–4 minutes.

Cut the duck breasts on the diagonal into thin slices. Fan the slices on warmed individual plates and spoon a little of the sauce over the top. Serve right away. Pass the remaining sauce in a warmed small bowl.

1 or 2 narrow strips orange zest, removed from the fruit with a vegetable peeler

Juice of 1 orange

2 shallots, minced

6 black peppercorns

½ cup (3 oz/90 g) dried tart cherries

1 tablespoon honey

2 tablespoons cold unsalted butter, cut into pieces

1 teaspoon cornstarch

SERVES 4

Crisp, browned duck skin is achieved by dousing the uncooked duck with boiling water, then with soy sauce, and refrigerating the duck for a day.

POMEGRANATE-GLAZED DUCK

1 whole Muscovy or Long Island duck, about 4–5 lb (2–2.5 kg), butterflied (see page 81)

6 cups (48 fl oz/1.5 l) boiling water

2 tablespoons soy sauce

FOR THE GLAZE

2 tablespoons pomegranate molasses

2 tablespoons soy sauce

1 clove garlic, finely grated

½ teaspoon finely grated and peeled fresh ginger

Chinese five-spice powder

SERVES 2 OR 3

Place the duck, skin side up, on a clean rack set in the sink. Pour 1–2 cups (8–16 fl oz/250–500 ml) of the boiling water evenly over the duck. Repeat 2 or 3 times, waiting 2 minutes between dousings. Pat the duck dry with paper towels and transfer the duck to a plate. Brush the duck skin with the soy sauce. Refrigerate, uncovered, for 24 hours to dry out the skin.

Remove the duck from the refrigerator about 30 minutes before roasting. Preheat the oven to 400°F (200°C).

Line a large rimmed baking sheet with heavy-duty aluminum foil. Select a flat roasting rack that will elevate the duck at least ½ inch (12 mm) off the bottom of the baking sheet. Oil the rack and set it in the prepared baking sheet.

To make the glaze, in a small bowl, stir together the pomegranate molasses, soy sauce, garlic, ginger, and a small pinch of the five-spice powder.

Place the duck, skin side up, on the oiled rack, spreading the legs away from the body to expose more skin. Pour 1 cup (8 fl oz/250 ml) water into the baking sheet. Roast the duck for 30 minutes. Remove the baking sheet from the oven and lightly brush the skin with the glaze. Using a bulb baster, carefully remove and discard as much of the accumulated hot liquid as possible from the bottom of the baking sheet. Continue to roast the duck until the skin is browned and crisp and a thermometer inserted into the thickest part of the thigh away from the bone registers 170° (77°C), about 30 minutes longer. Remove the baking sheet from the oven, transfer the duck to a carving board, and tent with aluminum foil. Let rest for 10 minutes.

Meanwhile, pour any remaining glaze into a small saucepan and bring it to a boil over high heat. Remove from the heat and set aside. Using a sharp, heavy knife or poultry shears, cut the duck in half along each side of the breastbone. Cut each half in half again, separating the breast and wing from the thigh and leg. Divide the duck among warmed individual plates. Pour the warm glaze over the duck meat and serve right away.

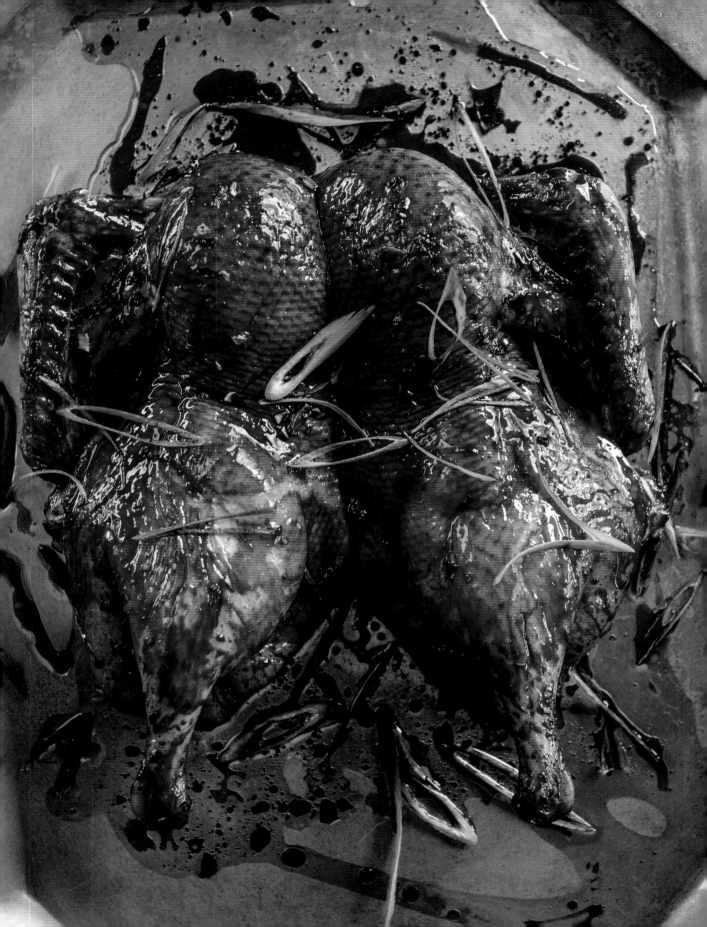

Roast goose is the traditional bird at many a Christmas table. The breast meat of a goose tends to dry out during roasting, so brining it for 24 hours helps keep it moist and succulent.

CHRISTMAS GOOSE WITH APPLE–DRIED FRUIT COMPOTE

1½ cups (12 oz/375 g) kosher salt, plus more for seasoning

¾ cup (6 oz/185 g) sugar

10 juniper berries, crushed

10 black peppercorns

1 cinnamon stick

1 young goose, about 10 lb (5 kg), with giblets

1 tart green apple, cored and chopped

1 small yellow onion, chopped

FOR THE COMPOTE

2 teaspoons extra-virgin olive oil

1 large shallot, minced

4 cups (32 fl oz/1 l) apple juice

1¼ cups (4 oz/125 g) dried apples

continued

In a large nonreactive container, combine 1½ cups (12 oz/375 g) salt with the sugar, and 6 cups (48 fl oz/1.5 l) room-temperature water. Stir until the salt and sugar dissolve. Add the juniper berries, peppercorns, and cinnamon stick, and stir to combine.

Remove the giblets and neck from the goose cavity; reserve the liver for another use or discard. Reserve the neck, gizzard, and heart for the roasting pan. Remove any excess fat from the cavity and reserve for another use or discard. Trim the neck skin, leaving just enough to fold over and skewer. Immerse the goose, breast side down, in the brine. If needed, invert a small plate on top of the goose to keep it submerged. Cover the container with plastic wrap and refrigerate for 24 hours.

Remove the goose from the brine and rinse it under cold running water. Pat the goose dry with paper towels and let stand at room temperature for 1 hour before roasting.

Preheat the oven to 375°F (190°C). Place a V-shaped roasting rack in a roasting pan large enough to hold the goose.

Holding the blade of a sharp knife almost parallel to the skin, make small slits in the skin over the breast and thighs. Do not cut into the meat. Sprinkle the cavity with pepper and place the apple and the onion in the cavity. Pierce 3 metal trussing or poultry pins through the skin from one side of the cavity to the opposite side, making sure they are parallel and evenly spaced. Lace a piece of kitchen string around the pins, as if lacing a shoe, pulling it tight to close the cavity. Knot the string and trim any excess. Tie the legs together with kitchen string. Tuck the wing tips under the back and tie a piece of kitchen string around the breast and wings. Transfer the goose, breast side up, to the rack. In a saucepan, bring 4 cups (32 fl oz/1 l) water to a boil and pour it into the bottom of the roasting pan. Add the giblets and neck. Cover the pan with aluminum foil. Place the goose in the oven and steam-roast for 45 minutes. Remove the foil from the pan and, using a small ladle, baste the goose with the liquid in the bottom of the pan. Continue to roast the goose uncovered, basting occasionally with the liquid, until a thermometer inserted into the thickest part of a thigh registers 170°F (77°C), about 2 hours. If the goose is getting too brown, cover the breast with foil.

Meanwhile, make the compote: In a large saucepan over medium-low heat, warm the oil. Add the shallot and sauté until very soft, 4–5 minutes. Add the apple juice, dried apples, cherries, raisins, orange peel and juice, ginger, mustard, and cinnamon. Bring the mixture to a boil over high heat, reduce the heat to low, and simmer until the fruit is plumped and softened, 20–25 minutes. If there is a lot of unabsorbed liquid, in a small bowl, dissolve the cornstarch in 1 tablespoon water, then stir the mixture into the fruit and cook, stirring occasionally, until slightly thickened, 2–3 minutes. Remove from the heat and set aside.

When the goose is done, transfer it to a carving board and tent with aluminum foil. Let rest for 20 minutes.

Meanwhile, make the sauce: Strain the contents of the roasting pan through a fine-mesh sieve into a saucepan. Spoon off as much fat as possible from the surface and reserve it for another use or discard. Add the stock and vermouth to the pan, place over high heat, and bring to a boil. Boil until reduced to about 1 cup (8 fl oz/250 ml), about 6 minutes. In a small bowl, dissolve the cornstarch in 2 tablespoons water and add to the pan. Continue to cook, stirring occasionally, until slightly thickened, about 2 minutes. Season to taste with salt and pepper and keep warm.

Carve the goose, cutting the thighs from the drumsticks and slicing the meat from each thigh. Arrange the goose on a warmed platter and serve with the fruit compote, warmed or at room temperature, and pass the sauce at the table.

⅓ cup (2 oz/60 g) pitted dried tart cherries

⅓ cup (2 oz/60 g) golden raisins

1 large strip orange peel, stuck with 2 whole cloves

Juice of 1 orange

1 teaspoon grated and peeled fresh ginger

½ teaspoon dry mustard

¼ teaspoon ground cinnamon

1½ teaspoons cornstarch, if needed

FOR THE SAUCE:

2 cups (16 fl oz/500 ml) chicken stock or low-sodium broth

⅓ cup (3 fl oz/80 ml) dry vermouth or dry white wine

1 tablespoon cornstarch

Kosher salt and freshly ground pepper

SERVES 6

SEAFOOD

FISH

ALBACORE TUNA WITH
WARM TOMATO, BASIL
& CAPER SALSA 132

ROSTED FISH FILLETS WITH
SUMMER VEGETABLES 133

BLACK PEPPER HALIBUT
STEAKS WITH ROASTED
TOMATOES 134

COD WITH POTATOES
& AIOLI 136

SEA BASS WITH FENNEL 137

FISH ROASTED WITH
SHIITAKE MUSHROOMS 139

WHOLE ROASTED SALMON
WITH HERB BUTTER
& TOMATOES 140

SALMON WITH MUSHROOM-
WINE SAUCE 141

SALMON WITH LEEKS,
FENNEL & LEMON 142

TROUT WITH HORSERADISH
BREAD CRUMBS 146

SALT-ROASTED WHOLE
FISH FOR TWO WITH
FRESH DILL SAUCE 149

ROASTED BRANZINO WITH
HERBED FARRO 151

SHELLFISH

CLAMS WITH POTATOES,
SAUSAGE & RED PEPPER 153

PAN-ROASTED MUSSELS
WITH FENNEL SEEDS,
SAFFRON & BASIL 154

SPICY MARINATED
SHRIMP 157

ROASTED SHRIMP WITH
TWO SAUCES 158

ROASTED LOBSTER WITH
TARRAGON BUTTER 159

SEAFOOD FOR ROASTING

Nearly every type of fish and shellfish is suitable for roasting. A whole fish stays moist and flavorful in the high heat of an oven, and steaks and fillets take just minutes to cook. Searing steaks and fillets on the stove top before briefly roasting browns their exterior, which adds a layer of deep flavor. The relatively small size of shellfish means that they are well suited to high-temperature roasting, which will caramelize their exterior in the short amount of time that it takes them to cook through.

Unlike meat and poultry, fish inspections have no federal standards in the U.S., nor is there a grading system. Shellfish, however, are inspected to ensure that they come from clean waters. To be sure that you are buying quality seafood, get to know a local fishmonger who has a high-volume business and is comfortable answering questions about their products. Whenever possible, smell your fish and shellfish before you purchase it to determine if it is fresh.

WHOLE FISH

CHOOSING Avoid fish with sunken eyes. The gills should be bright red, not brick red. Choose fish that are relatively thick for their length; they will roast better and have a higher yield. Ask the fishmonger to clean and scale the fish before wrapping it.

PREPPING If the gills are still intact, lift the gill flaps and clip out the gills with kitchen shears. Rinse the fish well inside and out under cold running water, then pat the fish very dry with paper towels.

STORING Whenever possible, cook whole fish the same day you buy it. If you must, refrigerate whole fish in a baking dish, packed in ice.

FISH FILLETS & STEAKS

CHOOSING Select fish that looks moist and feels firm. For dark-meat fish, such as tuna, avoid fillets or steaks that have an iridescent sheen.

PREPPING Run your finger down the surface of a fillet to locate any pin bones hidden in the flesh. If you find bones, pull them out with clean needle-nosed pliers or tweezers.

STORING Whenever possible, cook fish the same day you buy it. If you must, refrigerate the wrapped packages in a baking pan and cover with ice. Do not let the flesh of the fish come in contact with the ice.

SHELLFISH

CHOOSING Bivalve mollusks must be purchased live. Check them carefully; their shells should be free of cracks and tightly closed, or close tightly to the touch. Look for untreated or "dry" scallops that look creamy in color. Live lobsters should be stored in clean tanks and appear lively. Shrimp should feel firm to the touch, have a clean, fresh smell, and be free of black spots.

PREPPING Scrub bivalve mollusks well under cold running water with a sturdy brush. Devein shrimp, if desired, and then rinse under running cold water. Pull off the small white muscle attached to the side of scallops. Follow the directions in the recipe for lobster.

STORING For best results, cook all types of fresh shellfish on the same day that you purchase them. Keep all shellfish refrigerated until you are ready to cook. Remove live clams or mussels from their packaging, place them in a bowl, cover completely with a moist kitchen towel, and refrigerate.

HOW TO ROAST SEAFOOD

1 PREP

Unlike meats and poultry, it is not necessary to bring seafood to room temperature before roasting. In fact, you should keep it cold until you are ready to cook. Prep the seafood according to the recipe. Preheat the oven to the desired temperature.

2 FLAVOR

Flavor the seafood as directed, sprinkling it with spices, a marinade, a bread crumb mixture, or other savory flavorings.

3 BROWN

Some recipes may call for browning before the seafood goes into the oven. Be sure to choose a sturdy, ovenproof pan that can withstand high heat.

4 ROAST

Put the seafood in the oven and let it roast, paying attention to the cues in the recipe for turning or glazing as needed.

5A CHECK FISH

In general, the timing for fish is 10 minutes per inch (2.5 cm) of thickness. If you are roasting a whole fish, measure it at its thickest point. If there are additional items in the roasting pan, such as vegetables, the fish will take a bit longer. Check fish for doneness by inserting a knife into it and checking that it is just opaque (dark-meat fish, like tuna or salmon, can be cooked less, and the flesh of these varieties may not be opaque).

5B CHECK SHELLFISH

Follow the cues in the recipes to gauge the doneness of shellfish. Seafood cooks quickly, so be sure to check it for doneness before the suggested cooking time in order to prevent overcooking. Bivalve mollusks are done as soon as the shells pop open. Shrimp and scallops are ready to serve when they are just opaque.

6 SERVE

Serve seafood as soon as you can after cooking. If you are making a companion sauce or topping, try to complete it before or while the seafood is in the oven.

BONING A FISH FILLET

Even when you buy fish fillets from a fishmonger,
it's always a good idea to check for errant bones.

1 FIND THE BONES

Lay a fillet on a cutting board skin side down. Run a fingertip along the fillet near the center. If you feel the tips of bones sticking up, the pin bones are still in place.

2 PULL OUT THE BONES

Using fish tweezers or needle-nose pliers, pull out the bones one by one, gripping the tip of each bone and pulling up diagonally.

PEELING & DEVEINING SHRIMP

For the best quality, purchase whole shrimp from a seafood shop
with a good reputation and peel and devein them just before cooking.

1 PULL OFF THE SHELL

Pull off the small legs on the underside of a shrimp. Starting at the head of the shrimp, pull away the shell sections, leaving the tail section intact, if desired.

2 EXPOSE THE VEIN

Using a paring knife, make a shallow cut along the outer curve almost to the tail of each shrimp.

3 REMOVE & RINSE

With the tip of the knife, lift out the vein and pull it away, gently scraping it if necessary. Rinse the shrimp well.

ALBACORE TUNA WITH WARM TOMATO, BASIL & CAPER SALSA

4 albacore tuna steaks

Kosher salt and freshly ground pepper

3 tablespoons olive oil

3 tablespoons finely chopped red onion

1½ cups (9 oz/280 g) chopped, seeded, ripe tomatoes

2 tablespoons balsamic vinegar

1 tablespoon capers, roughly chopped

8 fresh basil leaves, cut into thin slivers

SERVES 4

Meatlike tuna steaks take well to a variety of different flavors. Here, they're quickly roasted and then topped with a warm summer salsa of fresh, ripe tomatoes, piquant capers, and garden basil.

Preheat the oven to 400°F (200°C).

Pat the tuna fillets dry with paper towels. Brush the fillets with 1 tablespoon of the oil, season both sides with salt and pepper, and place on a rimmed baking sheet. Roast the fish until opaque throughout, 15–20 minutes.

Meanwhile, in a frying pan over medium-low heat, warm the remaining 2 tablespoons oil. Add the onion and sauté until softened, about 2 minutes. Add the tomatoes, vinegar, and capers, and season to taste with salt and pepper. Cook, stirring occasionally, until the mixture is warmed through, about 2 minutes. Stir in the basil.

Divide the tuna among warmed individual plates. Spoon the warm salsa over the fish, dividing evenly, and serve right away.

This easy recipe highlights the best of summer produce in a one-pan meal. Be sure to select thick fish fillets, which stay moist in the high heat of the oven.

In a saucepan of boiling water, cook the potatoes until tender, when pierced with the tip of a paring knife, about 20 minutes. Drain and let cool. Peel and cut into thin slices.

Preheat the oven to 400°F (200°C). Choose a baking dish that will hold the fillets in a single layer and brush with ½ tablespoon of the oil.

Rinse the fillets under cold running water and pat dry with paper towels. Arrange the fillets skin side down in the prepared dish and sprinkle lightly with salt and pepper. Arrange the potato slices in overlapping rows on top of the fish. Create a row of tomato and zucchini slices down the center of the fish, alternating the vegetables. Scatter the onion over the top and drizzle with the remaining 1½ tablespoons oil. Season the vegetables lightly with salt and pepper and roast until the fish flakes easily when prodded with a fork and is opaque throughout when pierced with a knife, about 35 minutes. Remove from the oven, sprinkle with the chopped basil, and serve right away, directly from the dish.

ROASTED FISH FILLETS WITH SUMMER VEGETABLES

1 lb (500 g) Yukon gold potatoes, unpeeled

2 tablespoons olive oil

2 lb (500 g) skin-on cod fillets

Kosher salt and freshly ground pepper

1 ripe tomato, thinly sliced

1 zucchini, thinly sliced on the diagonal

1 small yellow onion, sliced

2 tablespoons chopped fresh basil

SERVES 6

Crusted with coarsely crushed black pepper, steak au poivre is a classic preparation for beef, but it's also a delicious and bold way to flavor meaty fish steaks. Here, the seasoned fish is roasted on a bed of sliced tomatoes, which are served alongside.

BLACK PEPPER HALIBUT STEAKS WITH ROASTED TOMATOES

6 halibut steaks, each about ¾-inch (2-cm) thick

2–3 tablespoons unsalted butter, melted

1 teaspoon black peppercorns, crushed

2 large tomatoes, sliced

¼ cup (¼ oz/7 g) lightly packed fresh basil leaves

SERVES 6

Preheat the oven to 400°F (200°C).

Rinse the halibut steaks under cold running water and pat dry with paper towels. Brush the fish with enough of the melted butter to coat. Sprinkle with the pepper and press gently so the pepper adheres to the fish.

Arrange the tomato slices in a single layer in a buttered baking dish just large enough to hold the fish in a single layer, and arrange the basil leaves, then the fish, on top of the tomatoes. Roast until the halibut flakes easily when gently prodded with a fork, 8–10 minutes.

Using a spatula, transfer the halibut steaks and tomatoes to warmed individual plates and serve right away.

Cod, potatoes, and aioli are a classic combination. The aioli can be made up to 1 day in advance and refrigerated until serving. You will need to start roasting the potatoes about 20 minutes before adding the cod to the pan.

COD WITH POTATOES & AIOLI

FOR THE AIOLI

1 large egg

4 cloves garlic, minced

1 teaspoon fresh lemon juice

1 teaspoon white wine vinegar

1 teaspoon Dijon mustard

2 or 3 drops green jalapeño chile sauce

Kosher salt and freshly ground pepper

½ cup (4 fl oz/125 ml) canola oil

¼ cup (2 fl oz/60 ml) extra-virgin olive oil, plus more as needed

1 lb (500 g) fingerling potatoes, unpeeled

2 cod fillets, each 12–14 oz (375–440 g) and about 1 inch (2.5 cm) thick

Sweet paprika

SERVES 4

To make the aioli, in a food processor, combine the egg, garlic, lemon juice, vinegar, mustard, chile sauce, 1 tablespoon kosher salt and a few grinds of pepper until blended. Combine the canola oil and ¼ cup (2 fl oz/60 ml) olive oil in a measuring pitcher. With the motor running, add the oils to the food processor in a slow, steady stream until the mixture thickens to the consistency of mayonnaise.

Preheat the oven to 400°F (200°C). Line a large rimmed baking sheet with heavy-duty aluminum foil.

In a bowl, toss the potatoes with 1 tablespoon olive oil, then sprinkle with salt and pepper. Arrange the potatoes on half of the prepared baking sheet. Roast the potatoes until the blade of a knife goes in fairly easily but the potatoes are still a little firm, 20–25 minutes.

Meanwhile, rinse the fillets under cold running water and pat them dry with paper towels. Lightly brush or rub both sides with olive oil, then sprinkle both sides with salt and pepper. Lightly sprinkle one side with paprika.

Remove the baking sheet from the oven and place the fillets, paprika side up, on the empty half of the baking sheet. Roast the fish with the potatoes, without turning, until the fish flakes easily when gently prodded with a fork and is opaque at the center when tested with a knife, 8–10 minutes. Transfer the fish to a carving board.

Cut each fish fillet into 2 pieces and arrange on individual warmed plates with the potatoes. Spoon the aioli into individual ramekins and place on each plate. Serve right away.

Individual gratin dishes filled with roasted fennel and juicy sea bass make a simple but elegant dish for a dinner party. Adding an anise-flavored liqueur, such as French Pernod, intensifies the fennel flavor.

SEA BASS WITH FENNEL

Preheat the oven to 400°F (200°C).

Quarter the fennel bulbs lengthwise and cut away the tough core. Divide among 4 individual gratin dishes. Brush the fennel with the oil, then sprinkle with salt and pepper. Roast until almost tender, about 20 minutes.

Meanwhile, rinse the fillets under cold running water and pat dry with paper towels. Place them in a baking dish just large enough to hold them in a single layer. Sprinkle with salt and pepper on both sides. In a small bowl, combine the 2 tablespoons oil, the Pernod, garlic, lemon zest, and lemon juice, then pour the mixture over the fish. Turn to coat the fish on both sides. Let stand at room temperature for about 20 minutes.

Use a spatula to divide the fillets among the gratin dishes, placing 1 fillet on top of each bed of fennel. Pour the remaining marinade over the fish. Roast until the fish is opaque throughout and the fennel is lightly browned and tender when pierced with a knife, about 10 minutes.

Finely chop some of the reserved fennel fronds and sprinkle them over the fish. Serve right away, passing the lemon wedges at the table.

3 fennel bulbs, 8–10 oz (250–315 g) each, trimmed, fronds reserved

2 tablespoons extra-virgin olive oil, plus extra for brushing

Kosher salt and freshly ground pepper

4 bluenose sea bass fillets, 6–8 oz (185–250 g) each

3 tablespoons Pernod or other anise-flavored liqueur

2 cloves garlic, minced

Grated zest of 1 lemon

1 tablespoon fresh lemon juice

Lemon wedges, for serving

SERVES 4

Packed with umami, shiitake mushrooms add a savory, meaty quality to simply roasted fish. Rather than rinsing, gently brush the mushrooms with a soft brush or damp cloth. Remove and discard the stems before using. Try this recipe with salmon fillets, too.

FISH ROASTED WITH SHIITAKE MUSHROOMS

Preheat the oven to 400°F (200°C).

Rinse the fillets under cold running water and pat dry with paper towels. Sprinkle them with the paprika and salt and pepper. Pour the oil and wine into a baking dish large enough to hold the fillets in a single layer. Scatter the garlic over the bottom of the dish and place the fillets, then the mushrooms, on top.

Roast for 15 minutes. Baste the mushrooms and fish with the pan juices. Continue to cook, basting once or twice, until the sea bass is opaque throughout when gently prodded with a fork, about 5 minutes longer. Garnish with the green onions and serve right away, directly from the dish.

1¾ lb (875 g) skinless sea bass fillets

2 teaspoons hot paprika

Kosher salt and freshly ground pepper

2 tablespoons olive oil

2 tablespoons dry white wine

3 cloves garlic, minced

¾ lb (375 g) shiitake mushrooms, brushed clean, stemmed, and sliced

4 green onions, including tender green parts, thinly sliced on the diagonal

SERVES 4

Here is a simple but refreshing summer dish that is perfect for an al fresco party with friends. To seed the tomatoes, halve them crosswise and gently squeeze out the seeds and the juice.

WHOLE-ROASTED SALMON WITH HERB BUTTER & TOMATOES

FOR THE HERB BUTTER

½ cup (4 oz/125 g) unsalted butter, cut into tablespoon-sized pieces, at room temperature

2 tablespoons fresh dill or tarragon leaves

2 tablespoons white wine vinegar

Kosher salt and freshly ground pepper

1 whole salmon, 4–5 lb (2–2.5 kg), cleaned and head removed

Olive oil, for coating

Kosher salt and freshly ground pepper

4 fresh tarragon sprigs

2 tomatoes, seeded and chopped (about 9 oz/280 g)

1 small yellow onion, chopped

SERVES 6–8

To make the herb butter, in a food processor, combine the butter, dill, and vinegar, and process for a few seconds, just until the ingredients are combined. Spoon into a small bowl and season to taste with salt and pepper. Cover, or form into a log in waxed paper, and refrigerate for at least 30 minutes or up to 3 days. Bring to room temperature before serving.

Preheat the oven to 450°F (230°C).

Rinse the salmon under cold running water and pat dry with paper towels. Put the salmon in a large oiled baking dish. Coat the fish with olive oil and season it inside and out with salt and pepper. Put the tarragon sprigs inside the fish.

In a bowl, toss together the tomatoes and onion; top the salmon with the tomato mixture.

Roast the salmon until the flesh flakes easily when gently prodded with a fork, 20–25 minutes.

Remove the salmon from the oven and let rest for 10 minutes. Using 2 spatulas, carefully transfer the salmon to a warmed platter and surround it with the tomato mixture.

To serve, peel back the skin of the fish, if desired, and cut the fish crosswise. Top the individual servings with pats of tarragon butter and serve right away.

Searing salmon helps it stand up to red wine, and the wine's acidity counters the oiliness of the fish; just be sure the wine is low in tannin. Mushrooms are a great bridge ingredient.

SALMON WITH MUSHROOM-WINE SAUCE

Preheat the oven to 450°F (230°C).

Prepare the mushrooms: If using shiitake mushrooms, remove and discard the stems. Brush all the mushrooms clean, then trim and cut them into ¾-inch (2-cm) pieces. This may mean keeping small mushrooms whole.

In a large frying pan over medium-high heat, melt the butter. Add the shallots and sauté until they starts to soften, about 30 seconds. Add the mushrooms, tarragon, parsley, ½ teaspoon salt, and a few grinds of pepper. Sauté until the mushrooms have softened, 2–3 minutes. Add the wine, cover, reduce the heat to low, and cook, stirring once or twice, until the mushrooms are tender, about 10 minutes. Stir in the vinegar and simmer, uncovered, for 1 minute longer to blend the flavors. Remove from the heat.

Rinse the fillets under cold running water and pat dry with paper towels. Sprinkle the salmon on both sides with salt and pepper. Heat a large, heavy ovenproof frying pan over high heat for 2–3 minutes. Add the oil and swirl to coat the pan. Place the salmon fillets, skinned side down, in the pan and sear for 2 minutes. Transfer the pan to the oven and roast until the salmon is lightly firm to the touch and is opaque throughout when tested with a knife, about 6 minutes.

Divide the salmon among warmed individual plates, and spoon the mushrooms on top, dividing evenly. Serve right away.

1 lb (500 g) assorted fresh mushrooms, such as shiitake, cremini, oyster, or chanterelle

3 tablespoons unsalted butter

2 tablespoons minced shallots

2 tablespoons chopped fresh tarragon

2 tablespoons chopped fresh flat-leaf parsley

Kosher salt and freshly ground pepper

¼ cup (2 fl oz/60 ml) Pinot Noir

2 teaspoons sherry vinegar

4 skinless salmon fillets, about 6 oz (185 g) each

2 teaspoons canola oil

SERVES 4

In this fast and easy main course, salmon, leeks, and fennel are roasted together. Serve with roasted or mashed potatoes for a complete meal. The recipe can easily be increased to serve additional guests.

SALMON WITH LEEKS, FENNEL & LEMON

3 tablespoons extra-virgin olive oil, plus more for greasing

3 fennel bulbs, 8–10 oz (250–315 g) each

4 or 5 large leeks, including 1 inch (2.5 cm) of tender green part, thinly sliced

Kosher salt and freshly ground pepper

6 skin-on salmon fillets, 6–7 oz (185–220 g) each

1 teaspoon fresh thyme leaves

Juice of 1 lemon

SERVES 6

Preheat the oven to 425°F (220°C). Lightly oil a rimmed baking sheet with olive oil.

Cut off the stems and fronds from the fennel bulbs. Finely chop the fronds from 1 bulb and reserve the fronds from another for garnish. Discard the remaining fronds and any stems. Cut each fennel bulb in half lengthwise and trim away the tough core. Cut the bulbs crosswise into thin slices.

Scatter about half the leeks and half the sliced fennel bulbs evenly over the bottom of the prepared baking sheet. Lightly season with salt and pepper. Rinse the fillets under cold running water and pat dry with paper towels. Arrange the fillets, skin side down, on top of the vegetables. Season with salt, pepper, half of the thyme, and about ⅓ cup (⅓ oz/10 g) of the chopped fennel fronds. Drizzle the fillets with half of the lemon juice and 1½ tablespoons oil.

Roast the salmon until opaque throughout when pierced with a knife, about 20 minutes, depending on the thickness of the fish; allow about 10 minutes for each inch (2.5 cm).

Meanwhile, toss the remaining chopped leeks and fennel bulbs in a baking dish with the remaining thyme, chopped fennel fronds, lemon juice, and 1½ tablespoons oil. Sprinkle with salt and pepper and transfer to the oven. Roast the vegetables alongside the fish until the vegetables are lightly browned and tender, about 15 minutes.

Using a spatula, transfer the leeks to a warmed platter and top with the salmon. Garnish with the reserved fennel fronds. Serve right away.

If you ever find whole, fresh trout at your fishmonger's, snap it up to make this simple, flavor-packed dish. You need just five primary ingredients and about 30 minutes of hands-on time to create this memorable dinner-party dish. Serve with roasted asparagus and sparkling wine.

TROUT WITH HORSERADISH BREAD CRUMBS

FOR THE HORSERADISH BREAD CRUMBS

2 cups (8 oz/250 g) dried white bread crumbs

6 tablespoons (3 oz/90 g) unsalted butter, melted

2 tablespoons prepared horseradish or grated fresh horseradish

2 tablespoons minced fresh chives

6 whole small rainbow trout, ¾–1 lb (375–500 g) each, cleaned

2 tablespoons unsalted butter, melted

Kosher salt and freshly ground pepper

3-inch (7.5-cm) chive lengths for garnish

SERVES 6

Preheat the oven to 450°F (230°C).

To make the horseradish crumbs, in a bowl, toss the bread crumbs with the butter, horseradish, and chives.

Rinse the trout under cold running water and pat dry with paper towels. Make 3 deep diagonal cuts on one side of each trout. Coat a large baking dish with the melted butter. Coat the trout with most of the melted butter and sprinkle to taste with salt and pepper. Arrange the trout, cut side up, in the pan. Sprinkle with the crumb mixture, spreading it evenly and gently pressing it into the cuts.

Roast the trout until the crumbs are lightly browned and the fish flakes easily when prodded gently with a fork, 15–20 minutes. Transfer to a warmed platter, garnish with the chive lengths, and serve right away.

Roasting a whole fish in a salt crust produces a juicy, flavorful result that is also healthful and low in fat. The crust is made by mixing together salt, beaten egg whites, and water to form a stiff mixture. The salt crust firms and hardens during the roasting, so you will need a mallet or small hammer to crack it in several places before it can be lifted from the fish. This recipe can easily be doubled for an impressive dinner party dish.

Preheat the oven to 400°F (200°C). Line a large rimmed baking sheet with heavy-duty aluminum foil.

Rinse the fish under cold running water and pat dry with paper towels. Brush the skin with oil and season the cavity with salt. Place the lemon slices, 2 of the bay leaves, the thyme sprigs, the green onion, and the peppercorns in the cavity.

To make the salt crust, pour the salt into a large bowl. In a small bowl, whisk together the egg whites and 1/3 cup (3 fl oz/80 ml) water until frothy. Add the egg white mixture to the salt and stir until the mixture holds together when pressed into a cake, adding a little more water if needed. Form a bed of the salt mixture about 1/2 inch (12 mm) thick on the prepared baking sheet, making it just large enough to hold the fish. Lay the remaining 4 bay leaves in a line down the length of the salt, then place the fish on the salt bed. Spoon the remaining salt mixture, a little at a time, onto the fish, pressing down on each addition to compact it before adding more. The fish should be covered with salt, although it is not necessary to cover the tail completely. Roast the fish for 25 minutes. *continued*

SALT-ROASTED WHOLE FISH FOR TWO WITH FRESH DILL SAUCE

1 whole striped bass, tilapia, or rockfish, about 2 lb (1 kg), cleaned

Extra-virgin olive oil, for brushing

Kosher salt

6 thin lemon slices

6 dried bay leaves

3 fresh thyme sprigs

1 green onion, cut into 2-inch (5-cm) lengths

4 black peppercorns

FOR THE SALT CRUST

6 cups (2 lb/1 kg) kosher salt

4 large egg whites

continued

SERVES 2

FOR THE DILL SAUCE

**1/2 cup (4 gl oz/125 ml)
crème fraîche or
sour cream**

**1/2 cup (4 oz/125 g)
plain yogurt**

3 teaspoons lemon juice

**2 tablespoons minced
fresh dill**

**Kosher salt and freshly
ground pepper**

Meanwhile, make the dill sauce: In a small bowl, combine the crème fraîche, yogurt, lemon juice, and dill. Season to taste with salt and pepper. Stir to blend. Cover and refrigerate until ready to serve.

Remove the pan from the oven and let the fish rest for 5 minutes. Using a mallet, firmly tap the salt crust to break it into several pieces. Using a heavy knife, cut off the head and the tail. Remove and discard the salt crust. Starting near the center of the back, use a thin-bladed knife to loosen the top fillet from the backbone. Then, using a spatula, transfer it to a warmed individual plate, skin side up. Remove the skin with a table knife and discard. Lift out and discard the backbone, then remove and discard the contents of the cavity. Transfer the bottom fillet to a second warmed plate, again discarding the skin. Serve right away, passing the dill sauce at the table.

Branzino, also known as Mediterranean sea bass, has a buttery flavor and silky texture. Here it is simply roasted with lemon and herbs, then paired with an herb- and lemon-flecked simmered farro.

ROASTED BRANZINO WITH HERBED FARRO

In a large saucepan over medium-high heat, combine the stock and farro and bring to a boil. Reduce the heat and simmer, covered, until the farro is tender but still pleasantly chewy, 25–30 minutes. Drain and set aside.

Preheat the oven to 450°F (230°C).

Zest the lemons, reserving the fruit. In a large frying pan, heat 2 tablespoons of the oil over medium heat. Add the onion, chopped herbs, and half of the lemon zest and sauté until the onion is softened. Add the drained farro, 1 teaspoon salt, and a generous grinding of pepper, and stir to mix . Reduce the heat to medium-low and cook until the farro is heated through, about 5 minutes. Stir in the remaining zest. Cover to keep warm and set aside.

Cut the reserved lemons into 20 thin slices. Rinse the fish under cold running water and pat dry with paper towels. Season the cavity and both sides of each fish with salt and pepper. Arrange the fish on an oiled large rimmed baking sheet. Place 2 lemon slices and a parsley sprig in each cavity. Lay 3 lemon slices along the top of each fish and finish with another parsley sprig. Drizzle each fish with 1 tablespoon oil.

Roast until sizzling and lightly golden on top, 10–15 minutes. The flesh should be flaky and white but still moist. Spoon the farro onto a large warmed platter and top with the roasted branzino. Drizzle with oil and serve right away.

4 cups (32 fl oz/1 l) chicken stock or low-sodium broth

1½ cups (10½ oz/330 g) farro, rinsed and drained

2 lemons

6 tablespoons (3 fl oz/90 ml) extra-virgin olive oil, plus more for greasing and drizzling

½ small red onion, finely chopped

¼ cup (⅓ oz/10 g) finely chopped fresh herbs, such as basil, mint, parsley, and thyme

Fine sea salt and freshly ground black pepper

4 whole branzino, about 1 lb (500 g) each, cleaned and gutted by the fishmonger

8 fresh flat-leaf parsley sprigs

SERVES 4

The combination of clams and chorizo is a classic in the traditional Spanish kitchen. It can be served as a first course, a light main course, or as part of a Spanish-style tapas meal. This recipe can easily be doubled; just be sure to roast the ingredients in a larger pan so that the vegetables can be spread out to brown evenly.

Preheat the oven to 425°F (220°C).

In a frying pan over medium-high heat, warm the oil. Add the sausage, breaking up the meat into small pieces. Cook, stirring occasionally, until the meat has no traces of pink, about 8 minutes. Set aside.

Scrub the clams well under cold running water. Discard any clams that do not close tightly to the touch.

Combine the potatoes, onion, bell pepper, and sausage in a heavy ovenproof frying pan with a lid. Drizzle with the remaining 3 tablespoons oil and sprinkle with the thyme and salt and pepper. Toss to coat, then spread them out in the pan in a single layer.

Roast, stirring once or twice, until the vegetables are sizzling and starting to brown around the edges, 30–35 minutes.

Remove the pan from the oven and pour in the stock. Add the clams, spreading them in a single layer. Cover the pan and roast until the clams open, 7–10 minutes. Remove from the oven and discard any that failed to open.

Spoon the mixture into warmed soup bowls or shallow pasta bowls. Sprinkle with the parsley and serve right away.

CLAMS WITH POTATOES, SAUSAGE & RED PEPPER

30 hard-shelled clams, such as manila clams

4 tablespoons (2 fl oz/60 ml) extra-virgin olive oil

2 fresh sweet or hot Italian sausages, casings removed

¾ lb (375 g) Yukon gold or fingerling potatoes, diced

1 small yellow onion, chopped

1 red bell pepper, seeded and chopped

½ teaspoon dried thyme

Kosher salt and freshly ground pepper

¼ cup (2 fl oz/60 ml) chicken stock or low-sodium broth

2 tablespoons chopped fresh flat-leaf parsley

SERVES 2

Mussels roast beautifully in a cast-iron pan in a hot oven, which surrounds them with heat and helps them cook quickly and evenly. Make sure that the mussels are very clean, so they don't mar the intensely flavored broth, which you'll want to sop up with grilled bread.

PAN-ROASTED MUSSELS WITH FENNEL SEEDS, SAFFRON & BASIL

2 lb (1 kg) large mussels, rinsed and debearded

2 tablespoons unsalted butter

2 tablespoons extra-virgin olive oil

4 cloves garlic, minced

Pinch of red pepper flakes

1/2 cup (4 fl oz/125 ml) dry white vermouth or wine

1 teaspoon fennel seeds, toasted

Pinch of saffron threads, toasted, and dissolved in 1 tablespoon hot water

1/3 cup (1/2 oz/15 g) finely shredded fresh basil leaves

Kosher salt

SERVES 4

Preheat the oven to 400°F (200°C).

Rinse the mussels under cold running water. Discard any that don't close to the touch.

In a large cast-iron frying pan or ovenproof sauté pan over medium heat, melt the butter with the olive oil until the butter foams. Add the garlic and red pepper flakes and sauté until fragrant, about 1 minute. Add the mussels, vermouth, fennel seeds, and the saffron mixture. Raise the heat to high and sauté for 30 seconds. Transfer the pan to the oven and roast until the mussels open, 4–6 minutes.

Remove from the oven and discard any mussels that failed to open. Sprinkle the mussels with the basil and season to taste with salt. Serve right away in the pan.

A simple but bold dish, these herb- and spice-coated shrimp take just seconds to put together. Set them out for a game-day treat; the recipe doubles easily to feed a crowd. If you are serving these as a main course, round out the plate with green beans and roasted potatoes.

In a nonreactive dish, toss the shrimp, garlic, thyme, red pepper flakes, half of the lemon juice, and 4 tablespoons (2 fl oz/60 ml) of the olive oil. Cover and refrigerate for at least 30 minutes or up to 1 hour.

Preheat the oven to 450°F (230°C).

Remove the shrimp from the marinade, and discard the marinade. Arrange the shrimp in a single layer on a rimmed baking sheet. Roast until they turn pink, begin to curl, and are tender, 7–8 minutes.

Transfer the shrimp to a serving platter and top with the remaining lemon juice. Season to taste with salt and serve right away.

SPICY MARINATED SHRIMP

1 lb (750 g) medium shrimp, peeled and deveined

2 large cloves garlic, minced

1 teaspoon dried thyme

1 teaspoon red pepper flakes

Juice of 2 lemons

6 tablespoons (3 fl oz/90 ml) olive oil

Kosher salt

SERVES 2–4

ROASTED SHRIMP WITH TWO SAUCES

FOR THE COCKTAIL SAUCE

²/₃ cup (5 fl oz/160 ml)
tomato ketchup

2 teaspoons prepared
horseradish

1 teaspoon *each* soy sauce
and fresh lemon juice

½ teaspoon balsamic
vinegar

½ teaspoon Worcestershire
sauce

¼ teaspoon dry mustard

Dash of hot-pepper sauce

FOR THE AVOCADO SAUCE

2 ripe avocados

1 tomato

1 small white onion

1 jalapeño chile

2 tablespoons fresh
lime juice

¼ teaspoon salt

24 tail-on jumbo shrimp,
peeled and deveined

⅓ cup (3 fl oz/80 ml)
hot-pepper sauce

2 teaspoons cumin seeds

SERVES 8

Roasting shrimp is easier than boiling it, and the high, dry heat helps intensify the naturally sweet flavors of the shellfish.

To make the cocktail sauce, in a small bowl, whisk together the ketchup, 1 teaspoon horseradish, the soy sauce, lemon juice, vinegar, Worcestershire sauce, mustard, and hot-pepper sauce until blended. Season to taste with more horseradish and hot-pepper sauce, if desired.

To make the avocado sauce, halve, pit, and chop the avocado. Peel and chop the tomato and onion. Seed and finely chop the jalapeño. In a food processor, combine the avocados, tomato, onion, chile, lime juice, and salt, and pulse to form a chunky purée. Spoon the mixture into a bowl, cover, and set aside.

Preheat the oven to 400°F (200°C).

Line a small baking sheet with aluminum foil and oil the foil. Arrange the shrimp in a single layer on the prepared sheet, toss with the hot-pepper sauce, and sprinkle with the cumin seeds.

Roast the shrimp, turning once, until they are evenly pink and firm to the touch, 3–3½ minutes on each side. Shrimp cook quickly, so be careful not to overcook them. Arrange the shrimp on a platter and serve right away, accompanied by the sauces.

The high heat of the oven intensifies the natural sweetness of lobster, which is nicely complemented by the verdant tarragon butter.

To make the tarragon butter, in a small bowl, mix the butter, tarragon, shallots, and lemon juice until blended. Season with salt and pepper. Cover and refrigerate until ready to use.

Fill a large stockpot with enough water to cover the lobsters and bring to a boil. Add the salt. Remove the lobsters from the refrigerator, leaving any rubber bands on the claws. Plunge the lobsters headfirst into the water. Cover the pot and listen carefully to determine when the water returns to a full boil; this could take 5 or 6 minutes. Once the water returns to a boil, cook the lobsters, covered, another 5 minutes. They will be half-cooked.

Using tongs, remove the lobsters from the pot and rinse under cold running water. Remove any rubber bands from the claws. To drain, plunge a knife into the head of each lobster between the eyes, and hold the lobster over the sink, holding it up first by the tail, then by the claws, and then by the tail again.

Turn each lobster on its back. If desired, remove the smaller legs. Using a chef's knife, cut each lobster in half vertically, from head to tail. Holding the tails at each end, bend the tails to crack them so that they will lie flat. Using a spoon, remove and discard the greenish sacs just below the heads. Remove and discard the intestinal tracts that run along the bottom of the shells from head to tail. Insert a long wooden skewer on one side of the large end of each lobster tail and push it to extend all the way through the tail to keep it flat while roasting. If desired, leave the tomalley and any roe.

Arrange 2 oven racks in the upper third and the center of the oven. Preheat to 425°F (220°C). Place 4 lobster halves, cut side up and facing opposite directions, on each of 2 baking sheets. Spread one-eighth of the tarragon butter over the cut side of each lobster half. Place the baking sheets in the oven and roast the lobster until the meat is opaque, about 5 minutes. Serve right away on large warmed plates, with lemon wedges for squeezing.

ROASTED LOBSTER WITH TARRAGON BUTTER

FOR THE TARRAGON BUTTER

½ cup (4 oz/125 g) unsalted butter, at room temperature

¼ cup (¼ oz/7 g) finely chopped fresh tarragon

2 shallots, minced

1 tablespoon fresh lemon juice

Kosher salt and freshly ground pepper

4 live Maine lobsters, 1¼–1½ lb (625–750 g) each

¼ cup (2 oz/60 g) kosher salt

Lemon wedges

SERVES 4

VEGETABLES & FRUIT

VEGETABLES & FRUIT FOR ROASTING

Roasting concentrates the flavors of vegetables and fruit, caramelizes their natural sugars, and tenderizes their interiors. As the heat from the oven penetrates to the center of each piece, the flavor deepens and the texture is transformed.

Some vegetables are better candidates than others for roasting, but many contenders exist. Sturdy root vegetables and tubers, such as beets, carrots, onions, parsnips, potatoes, and turnips, cook up beautifully in the dry heat of the oven. Cruciferous vegetables, such as broccoli, cauliflower, and brussels sprouts, roast exceptionally well. In the oven, their cabbagelike aromas are tamed and their strong flavors turn sweet and mellow. Delicate vegetables such as mushrooms, tomatoes, and summer squash, are also worthy of roasting, which brings out meaty or nutty flavors and sweetens any natural sugars that are present. Firm winter squash become creamy and yielding in the oven.

Fruit for roasting should be carefully chosen: Firm fruits with cores, like apples and pears, stone fruits like peaches, nectarines, and plums, and tropical fruits like pineapple will hold their shape during roasting. Many softer fruits, like berries, are not good candidates for roasting, because they can soften too much. When watched carefully, delicate figs and bananas emerge sweet and appealingly sticky from a hot oven.

VEGETABLES

CHOOSING For the best flavor and texture, choose vegetables that are at their seasonal peak. Roasting cannot bring out flavors that are not already present, so select produce that is ripe and naturally flavorful.

PREPPING Wash vegetables well, using a vegetable brush for especially dirty vegetables or those with edible skin. Cut vegetables into uniform pieces, as varying shapes and sizes will yield unevenly cooked food. With the exception of winter squash, smaller pieces are generally best when roasting vegetables, as they reduce the roasting time and allow for increased caramelization on their exposed surfaces.

STORING In general, try to cook vegetables within a few days of purchase. Most vegetables should be refrigerated until it's time to cook them. Tomatoes, potatoes, sweet potatoes, and whole winter squash can be stored at cool room temperature.

TESTING VEGETABLES & FRUITS FOR DONENESS

To test the doneness of roasted vegetables and fruits, first use your eyes: They should have an even, golden-brown color. Next, insert the tip of a sharp knife into a piece. In general, it should yield easily, but not be too soft, but you should also follow the cues in the recipe or your individual preference. If the vegetables have browned nicely but still need some more roasting, tent them loosely with foil and continue roasting.

FRUIT

CHOOSING For the best flavor and texture, choose fruit that are at their seasonal peak. Source your fruit from a farmers' market for in-season—and likely local—varieties.

PREPPING Wash fruit well to remove any residue. Cut fruit into uniform pieces to speed cooking and encourage caramelization.

STORING In general, try to cook fruit within a few days of purchase. Most fruit suitable for roasting (stone fruits, tropical fruits, and tree fruits) can be kept at room temperature. If the fruit starts to ripen too much, put it in the refrigerator.

HOW TO ROAST VEGETABLES & FRUIT

1 PREP

Cut large vegetables into uniform pieces. Some larger vegetables, like winter squash or large potatoes, can be halved.

2 COAT

Thoroughly coat the surface of the vegetables with oil or melted butter to encourage browning. Lightly season the vegetables and toss to coat.

3 ARRANGE

Put the vegetable pieces in a shallow pan that holds them in a single layer without crowding. If they are too snugly packed, you won't get the desired caramelized quality.

4 ROAST

Put the vegetables in the oven and let them roast. To check for doneness, inserting the tip of a paring knife into a piece to gauge tenderness.

In this irresistible take on stuffed artichokes, the vegetables are first boiled to soften their flesh, then they're filled with a bold mixture of bread crumbs, chiles, and fresh mint. They are finished in a hot oven, which brings out a naturally nutty quality in the artichokes and crisps the bread-crumb mixture that fills the leaves.

Bring a large pot of salted water to a boil. Halve the lemon, squeeze the juice into the boiling water, and carefully drop in the lemon halves. Using a sharp knife, cut off the top quarter of each artichoke, then trim the stem flush with the bottom. Using kitchen shears, cut the sharp tips off the leaves. Lower the artichokes into the boiling water and cook, turning occasionally, until the bottoms are almost tender when pierced with a knife and the leaves pull off easily, 15–20 minutes. Drain the artichokes upside down on a rack set over a baking sheet.

In a saucepan over medium heat, melt the butter with the 1 tablespoon oil. Add the onion and a pinch of salt and sauté until the onion is soft and translucent, 5–6 minutes. Add the chile, garlic, and red pepper flakes, and sauté for 2 minutes. Remove from the heat, stir in the bread crumbs, and transfer the mixture to a bowl. Add the egg and beat with a fork until the mixture is moistened. Stir in the mint and a generous pinch each of salt and pepper.

Preheat the oven to 350°F (180°C).

When cool enough to handle, gently open the artichoke leaves away from the center. Fill the cavity of each artichoke and the spaces between some of the leaves with the crumb mixture. Arrange the artichokes in a baking dish just large enough to hold them comfortably, and drizzle the tops with oil. Cover with aluminum foil and roast until the leaves pull off easily, about 20 minutes. Remove the foil and roast until the top of the filling is lightly browned, another 10 minutes.

Transfer the artichokes to warmed individual plates and serve right away.

STUFFED ARTICHOKES WITH SPICY HERBED BREAD CRUMBS

1 lemon

4 globe artichokes

1 tablespoon unsalted butter

1 tablespoon extra-virgin olive oil, plus additional for drizzling

1 yellow onion, finely diced

Kosher salt and freshly ground pepper

1 jalapeño chile, seeded and minced

2 cloves garlic, minced

$\frac{1}{2}$ teaspoon red pepper flakes

$1\frac{1}{2}$ cups (3 oz/90 g) fresh bread crumbs

1 large egg

$\frac{1}{2}$ bunch fresh mint leaves, thinly sliced

SERVES 4

Here's another wonderful way to serve asparagus, which is at its best in the spring. The tender stalks are tossed with olive oil, then topped with a mixture of bread crumbs, parsley, lemon zest, and Parmesan before roasting.

ASPARAGUS WITH PARMESAN BREAD CRUMBS

1 lb (500 g) asparagus, tough ends removed

2 tablespoons extra-virgin olive oil

1 cup (4 oz/125 g) grated Parmesan cheese

3 tablespoons dried bread crumbs

1 tablespoon minced fresh flat-leaf parsley

1 tablespoon grated lemon zest

2 tablespoons fresh lemon juice

Fine sea salt and freshly ground pepper

SERVES 4

Preheat the oven to 450°F (230°C).

Arrange the asparagus in a single layer in a baking dish and drizzle with half the oil. Toss the spears gently to coat.

In a bowl, stir together the cheese, bread crumbs, parsley, and lemon zest with 1 tablespoon lemon juice, $\frac{1}{2}$ teaspoon salt, and a pinch of pepper. Drizzle in the remaining 1 tablespoon oil and stir until mixed. Sprinkle the bread-crumb mixture over the asparagus and roast, uncovered, until the asparagus is just tender and the topping is melted and golden brown, 15 minutes.

Drizzle the asparagus with the remaining lemon juice and serve right away directly from the baking dish.

For best results, choose asparagus of the same thickness, preferably somewhat slim, to ensure that all the spears will cook evenly. To remove the tough end from each spear, bend the cut end of the spear until it breaks. It will naturally snap where the fibrous portion begins.

ASPARAGUS WITH SHALLOTS & LEMON

1 lb (500 g) asparagus, tough ends removed

2 tablespoons extra-virgin olive oil

2 tablespoons sliced shallot

Kosher salt and freshly ground pepper

2 teaspoons fresh lemon juice

1 teaspoon grated lemon zest

SERVES 4

Preheat the oven to 400°F (200°C).

Arrange the asparagus close together on a rimmed baking sheet. Brush the spears with the oil, turning to coat, and sprinkle the shallot evenly on top, then season generously with salt and pepper.

Roast the asparagus without turning, until the spears are tender and the tips are browned, 12–15 minutes.

Transfer the asparagus to a platter and sprinkle with the lemon juice and zest. Serve right away, warm, or at room temperature.

Stuffed with a savory-sweet filling, these sweet bell peppers can be offered as a vegetarian main course or a creative side for a party meal. Brown rice contributes a pleasant, chewy texture, but you could also opt for white rice, preferably an aromatic variety like jasmine or basmati.

ROASTED STUFFED RED PEPPERS

Preheat the oven to 425°F (220°C).

Using a serrated knife, cut off the top of each pepper, just low enough to reveal the ribs and seeds. Set the pepper tops aside. Using a spoon, scoop the ribs and seeds from the cavities of the peppers. Sprinkle the inside of each cavity generously with salt.

In a large frying pan, heat 1 tablespoon of the oil over medium-high. Add the onion and sauté until beginning to soften, about 3 minutes. Add the celery and carrot and sauté until softened, about 3 minutes. Stir in the mushrooms and garlic and sauté for 30 seconds. Stir in the rice, tomato, basil, and parsley. Remove from the heat and stir in the pine nuts and currants. Season to taste with salt and pepper.

Arrange the pepper shells cut side up in a baking dish just large enough to hold them comfortably. Spoon the rice mixture into the peppers, dividing it evenly; pack the rice lightly and mound it slightly on top. Replace the reserved tops. Drizzle the peppers with the remaining 3 tablespoons oil.

Roast until the skins begin to brown and just start to split, 20–30 minutes. Let cool slightly and serve right away.

6 uniformly shaped red bell peppers

Kosher salt and freshly ground pepper

¼ cup (2 fl oz/60 ml) olive oil

¾ cup (4 oz/125 g) finely chopped yellow onion

⅓ cup (2 oz/60 g) finely chopped celery

⅓ cup (2 oz/60 g) peeled and finely chopped carrot

¾ cup (2½ oz/75 g) finely chopped portobello mushrooms

2 cloves garlic, minced

3 cups (15 oz/470 g) cooked brown rice

1 tomato, seeded and chopped

2 tablespoons chopped fresh basil

2 tablespoons chopped fresh flat-leaf parsley

⅓ cup (1½ oz/45 g) pine nuts, toasted

½ cup (3 oz/90 g) dried currants

SERVES 6

Fennel has a strong, sweet anise flavor that pairs well with the assertive character of garlic. Because fennel can dry out easily during roasting, here it is drizzled with a little broth or wine to keep it moist while the edges caramelize. Serve this simple side dish with roasted pork, lamb, or fish.

GARLIC FENNEL WEDGES

Preheat the oven to 375°F (190°C).

Trim the stems from the fennel and reserve a few fronds for garnish. Trim away any bruised or tough outer layers. Cut the bulb lengthwise into wedges 1 inch (2.5 cm) wide, then remove the core. Combine the fennel and garlic on a rimmed baking sheet. Drizzle with the oil and stock and sprinkle generously with salt and pepper. Toss to coat. Arrange the wedges in a single layer.

Roast the fennel, stirring 1 or 2 times, for 20 minutes. Remove the pan from the oven and sprinkle the fennel evenly with the chopped thyme. Continue to roast until the fennel is browned at the edges and tender when pierced with a fork, another 25–30 minutes.

Remove the pan from the oven and transfer the fennel to a warmed serving bowl. Garnish with the reserved fennel fronds. Serve right away.

1 lb (500 g) fennel bulbs

4 large cloves garlic, sliced

3 tablespoons extra-virgin olive oil

2 tablespoons chicken stock, low-sodium chicken broth, or white wine

Kosher salt and freshly ground pepper

2 tablespoons chopped fresh thyme or oregano

SERVES 4

Crimson radicchio is a wonderful addition to salads, but it is also a terrific ingredient to grill or roast. Treated to high heat, the color mellows and the bitter flavor sweetens, while the leaves gain a tender texture that maintains some residual crunch. A sweet-sour vinaigrette and toasted walnuts lend savor and crunch.

GLAZED ROASTED RADICCHIO WITH WALNUTS

2 heads radicchio, about 10 oz (315 g) total weight

3 tablespoons balsamic vinegar

2 tablespoons olive oil

1 tablespoon walnut oil

1 tablespoon pure maple syrup

2 teaspoons chopped fresh thyme

Sea salt and freshly ground pepper

½ cup (2 oz/60 g) chopped walnuts

SERVES 4–6

Preheat the oven to 400°F (200°C).

Cut each radicchio head in half lengthwise. Trim away most of the core from each half, leaving just enough to keep the leaves attached, then cut each half lengthwise into 3 wedges. Arrange the wedges in a single layer in a roasting pan.

In a small bowl, whisk together the vinegar, olive oil, walnut oil, maple syrup, and thyme. Season to taste with salt and pepper. Pour the vinaigrette over the radicchio wedges and turn them to coat evenly.

Roast the radicchio cut side down for 10 minutes. Turn the radicchio and sprinkle the walnuts evenly over the top. Continue to roast until the wedges are tender and the outer leaves are crisped and browned, about 10 minutes longer. Transfer to a warmed serving platter or individual plates and spoon the walnuts and liquid from the roasting pan over the top. Serve right away, warm or at room temperature.

Intensely nutty hazelnuts echo the taste of butter cooked until rich golden brown. The deep flavor of the toasted nuts and brown butter pairs well with the earthy root vegetables, whose high level of natural sugars caramelizes when roasted. Fragrant thyme leaves impart an herbal depth to the dish.

In a small frying pan over medium-low heat, toast the nuts until they turn deep brown and the nuts smell fragrant, 5 minutes. While the nuts are still warm, wrap them in a clean kitchen towel. Rub the nuts vigorously to remove the skins (it is fine if some bits of skin remain). Transfer to a small bowl.

Preheat the oven to 425°F (220°C).

Drizzle half the oil onto each of 2 rimmed baking sheets. Place the sheets in the oven to preheat while you prepare the vegetables. Peel the parsnips and sweet potato, then cut them into pieces about ½ inch (12 mm) thick and 2–3 inches (5- to 7.5-cm) long. Remove the baking sheets from the oven and divide the vegetables between them. Sprinkle lightly with salt and pepper, toss the vegetables to coat with the oil, and arrange them in a single layer. Roast until the undersides are nicely browned and crisp, 10–12 minutes. Turn each piece over once or twice and roast until the vegetables are browned on all sides, another 8–10 minutes.

In the small frying pan, melt the butter over medium heat, stirring occasionally, until it begins to turn brown and smell nutty, 3–4 minutes. Remove the pan from the heat and stir in the hazelnuts and thyme.

Transfer the roasted vegetables to a large warmed bowl, drizzle with the brown butter mixture, and toss to coat. Season to taste with salt and pepper and serve right away.

ROOT VEGETABLES WITH HAZELNUTS & BROWN BUTTER

3 tablespoons coarsely chopped hazelnuts

3 tablespoons canola oil

1 lb (500 g) parsnips

1 lb (500 g) sweet potato

Kosher salt and freshly ground pepper

2 tablespoons unsalted butter

1 teaspoon minced fresh thyme

SERVES 4

These addictive savory, salty, sweet, and sour tomatoes are a versatile ingredient. Serve them as an accompaniment to roast beef or lamb, or as part of a picnic spread or pizza topping. They take a long time to cook, but it's unattended time, and it's a great way to make use of a glut of tomatoes from your garden crop.

SLOW-ROASTED TOMATOES

⅓ cup (3 fl oz/80 ml) olive oil, plus additional for greasing

12 plum tomatoes, halved lengthwise

2 cloves garlic, chopped

1 tablespoon fresh thyme leaves

2 teaspoons sugar

Kosher salt and freshly ground pepper

MAKES ABOUT 2½ CUPS (12 OZ/375 G)

Preheat the oven to 250°F (120°C).

Lightly oil a rimmed baking sheet. Arrange the tomatoes cut side up in a single layer on the prepared baking sheet. Drizzle the tomatoes with the ⅓ cup (3 fl oz/80 ml) oil. Sprinkle the garlic, thyme, sugar, 1 teaspoon salt, and ¼ teaspoon pepper evenly over the tomatoes. Place the tomatoes in the oven, and roast until lightly browned and wrinkled, about 3 hours.

Turn off the oven and let the tomatoes remain in the closed oven another 2 hours. Transfer the tomato halves to a shallow bowl and pour any pan juices over the top. Let cool, then use right away or refrigerate for up to 1 week.

With their dense texture and rich flavor, roasted portobello mushrooms make a satisfying vegetarian main course. You can also put the roasted caps between toasted slices of rustic country bread for a hearty sandwich, or slice them and stir them into a pan sauce for serving with roasted poultry or meats.

PORTOBELLO MUSHROOMS WITH PARMESAN & BASIL

Preheat the oven to 450°F (230°C).

Lightly oil a rimmed baking sheet. In a small bowl, whisk 2 tablespoons of the oil with the garlic. Brush the mushrooms all over with the garlic oil and sprinkle them with salt and pepper. Arrange the mushroom caps, gill side down, on the prepared pan. Roast for 10 minutes. Remove the pan from the oven, turn the mushrooms gill side up, and roast until tender when pierced with a fork, about 8 minutes.

Meanwhile, in a small dish, stir together the cheese and basil. Remove the pan from the oven and sprinkle with 2 tablespoons of the cheese mixture. Continue to roast until the cheese begins to melt, about 2 minutes.

In a small bowl, stir together the remaining 1 tablespoon oil and the vinegar. Remove the pan from the oven. Leave the mushrooms whole or cut into slices and arrange on warmed individual plates. Drizzle with the vinegar mixture, garnish each serving with a basil sprig, and sprinkle with the remaining cheese. Serve right away.

3 tablespoons extra-virgin olive oil, plus additional for greasing

1 large clove garlic, minced

4 large portobello mushrooms, about 6 oz (185 g) each, brushed clean, stems removed

Kosher salt and freshly ground pepper

¼ cup (4 oz/125 g) shaved Parmesan cheese

2 tablespoons thinly sliced fresh basil, plus 4 fresh sprigs

1 tablespoon sherry vinegar

SERVES 4

A quartet of spices commonly found in many Indian-style curry blends works magic on simple roasted beets. During cooking, the spice mixture perfumes the vegetables, and lingers even after the beets are peeled.

ROASTED BEETS WITH INDIAN SPICES

1 teaspoon ground cumin

1 teaspoon ground coriander

½ teaspoon ground turmeric

½ teaspoon ground cloves

Kosher salt and freshly ground pepper

6 beets, about 30 oz (940 g) total weight, stems trimmed to ½ inch (12 mm)

2 tablespoons olive oil

SERVES 4

Preheat the oven to 350°F (180°C).

In a small bowl, combine the cumin, coriander, turmeric, and cloves with 1 teaspoon salt, and 1 teaspoon pepper. Stir to mix.

Arrange the beets in a shallow roasting pan just large enough to hold them in a single layer. Drizzle them with the oil, then the spice mixture, turning to coat. Roast, turning occasionally, until the skins are slightly wrinkled and the beets are tender when pierced with a knife, about 1¼ hours.

When the beets are cool enough to handle, cut off the stems and peel them. Cut the beets lengthwise into wedges and serve right away, warm or at room temperature.

Small potatoes, simply roasted and tossed with chopped fresh herbs, are a versatile accompaniment to nearly any meal. Substitute small Yukon gold or fingerlings, if you like.

ROASTED RED POTATOES WITH SUMMER HERBS

¼ cup (2 fl oz/60 ml) extra-virgin olive oil

2 tablespoons fresh lemon juice

¼ teaspoon sweet paprika

Kosher salt and freshly ground pepper

2½ lb (1.25 kg) small red potatoes

1 tablespoon chopped fresh basil

1 tablespoon chopped fresh chives

SERVES 4–6

Preheat the oven to 425°F (220°C).

In a roasting pan, stir together the oil, lemon juice, paprika, and 1 teaspoon salt and ½ teaspoon pepper. Add the potatoes and toss to coat. Arrange the potatoes in a single layer and roast, turning often, until golden brown and tender when pierced with a knife, about 45 minutes.

Remove the potatoes from the oven and transfer to a warmed serving platter. Sprinkle with the basil and chives, and serve right away.

These garlic-flecked gems kick regular roasted potatoes up a notch. Be sure to add the garlic halfway through the cooking process. Add it at the beginning, and the garlic could burn.

FINGERLING POTATOES WITH GARLIC & THYME

Preheat the oven to 425°F (220°C).

In a large bowl, toss the potatoes with the oil and thyme. Sprinkle generously with salt and pepper.

Arrange the potatoes in a single layer on a rimmed baking sheet. Roast for 10 minutes, stir, and roast for another 10 minutes. Scatter the garlic on top of the potatoes and roast until the potatoes are golden brown and tender when pierced with a knife, about 10 minutes more.

Season the potatoes with salt and pepper and transfer to a warmed serving platter. Serve right away.

1 lb (500 g) small fingerling potatoes, halved lengthwise

¼ cup (2 fl oz/60 ml) extra-virgin olive oil

Leaves from 4 sprigs fresh thyme

Kosher salt and freshly ground pepper

3 cloves garlic, thinly sliced

SERVES 4

Waxy potatoes, such as those used here, retain their shape during roasting and have a dense, creamy texture when cooked. If you are roasting the potatoes along with meat or poultry and the oven temperature called for to accommodate the meat is 25°F (10°C) higher or lower than the temperature suggested here, the potatoes will still roast fine.

Preheat the oven to 400°F (200°C).

If the potatoes are larger than 1½ inches (4 cm) in diameter, cut them in half. Place the potatoes in a roasting pan and sprinkle with the rosemary. In a small bowl, stir together the oil and mustard. Drizzle the mixture evenly over the potatoes, then sprinkle generously with salt and pepper. Toss to coat the potatoes, then spread them out in a single layer.

Roast the potatoes, turning them 2 or 3 times, until the skin is golden and the flesh is tender when pierced with a knife, 40–45 minutes.

Remove the baking sheet from the oven. Transfer the potatoes to a warmed serving platter and serve right away.

HERBED POTATOES WITH WHOLE-GRAIN MUSTARD

1 lb (500 g) small red or Yukon gold potatoes

1 tablespoon chopped fresh rosemary

1 tablespoon extra-virgin olive oil

1 tablespoon whole-grain Dijon mustard

Kosher salt and freshly ground pepper

SERVES 4

Any variety of sweet potato works well for roasting because the natural sugars caramelize to a rich color and flavor, especially when augmented by a little molasses. The chili powder adds some heat to produce an appealing sweet-hot taste.

SWEET & SPICY SWEET POTATOES

1 lb (500 g) sweet potatoes, peeled, halved lengthwise, then sliced crosswise into half moons

3 tablespoons canola oil

1 tablespoon light or dark molasses

1 teaspoon chili powder

Kosher salt and freshly ground pepper

SERVES 4

Preheat the oven to 450°F (230°C).

Arrange the sweet potatoes in a single layer on a rimmed baking sheet. In a small bowl, whisk the oil and molasses. Drizzle the mixture over the sweet potatoes. Sprinkle with the chili powder, then sprinkle generously with salt and pepper. Toss to coat. Arrange the sweet potatoes in a single layer.

Roast the sweet potatoes, stirring 1 or 2 times, until they are browned and crisp and tender when pierced with a knife, 20–30 minutes.

Remove the baking sheet from the oven and transfer the potatoes to a warmed serving dish. Serve right away.

Festive enough for a holiday but fast enough for a snowy-day supper, these sweet potatoes will please a crowd, and the recipe is easily multiplied. You can also dress up the sweet spuds with spices like ground fennel or red pepper flakes.

MAPLE-GLAZED SWEET POTATO WEDGES

Preheat the oven to 450°F (230°C).

Cut the sweet potatoes lengthwise into uniform wedges about 1 inch (2.5 cm) wide. In a large bowl, whisk together the maple syrup, oil, rosemary, 1 teaspoon salt, and ½ teaspoon pepper. Add the sweet potato wedges and toss to coat.

Arrange the wedges in a single layer in a roasting pan and drizzle with any maple syrup mixture left in the bowl.

Roast for 20 minutes. Remove the pan from the oven and turn the wedges with a spatula or by shaking the pan, then continue roasting until tender when pierced with a knife, another 15 minutes. Season to taste with salt and pepper and transfer to a warmed serving platter. Serve right away.

3 sweet potatoes, about 1½ lb (750 g) total weight

2 tablespoons pure maple syrup

1 tablespoon olive oil

½ teaspoon chopped fresh rosemary

Kosher salt and freshly ground pepper

SERVES 4–6

Here's an easy way to enliven fresh zucchini: First, sprinkle it with olive oil and fresh thyme and roast it in a hot oven. While the zucchini cooks, prepare the potent three-ingredient topping made from anchovies, garlic, and olive oil, which provides a salty balance to the sweet zucchini. The dish goes well with lamb or fish.

ROASTED ZUCCHINI WITH ANCHOÏADE

6 zucchini

3 tablespoons olive oil

3 teaspoons fresh thyme leaves

Kosher salt and freshly ground pepper

FOR THE ANCHOÏADE

⅓–½ cup (3–4 fl oz/ 80–125 ml) extra-virgin olive oil

1 can (2½ oz/75 g) anchovy fillets, rinsed and drained

3 cloves garlic, minced

SERVES 4

Preheat the oven to 400°F (200°C).

Cut each zucchini in half crosswise, then cut each half lengthwise into 3 even slices. Arrange the slices in a roasting pan just large enough to hold them in a single layer. Drizzle with the olive oil and sprinkle with the thyme, ½ teaspoon salt, and several grinds of pepper.

Roast until the zucchini is golden brown on the underside, 15–20 minutes. Turn and roast until golden on the second side and tender-crisp when pierced with a fork, another 5–10 minutes.

Meanwhile, make the anchoïade: In a small frying pan over low heat, warm ⅓ cup (3 fl oz/80 ml) of the olive oil. Add the anchovies and garlic and cook, mashing the anchovies until they dissolve to make a paste, about 3 minutes. Gradually whisk in enough of the remaining oil to create the consistency of a thick vinaigrette. Keep warm.

Transfer the zucchini to a warmed serving platter. Serve it right away, accompanied by the anchoïade.

Despite their sturdy demeanor, root vegetables are rich in natural sugars, making them among the sweetest and gentlest in flavor of all the vegetables. A colorful assortment of uniformly chopped root vegetables creates a particularly attractive dish when roasted. You can adjust the amounts given here by using more of one vegetable than another or even using only a single vegetable. You can also substitute other herbs, such as sage or marjoram.

ROASTED ROOT VEGETABLE MEDLEY

Preheat the oven to 425°F (220°C).

Peel the carrots, parsnips, turnips, and celery root and cut into 1-inch (2.5-cm) pieces. Cut the unpeeled potatoes into 1-inch (2.5-cm) pieces. Combine the vegetables and garlic in a large, shallow roasting pan or on a rimmed baking sheet. Drizzle with the oil and sprinkle with 1½ tablespoons of the thyme. Season generously with salt and pepper. Toss to coat, and arrange the vegetables in a single layer.

Roast the vegetables for 10 minutes. Reduce the oven temperature to 350°F (180°C) and continue to roast them, stirring 1 or 2 times, until golden, caramelized, and tender when pierced with a knife, 35–45 minutes longer.

Remove the pan from the oven and season the vegetables to taste with salt and pepper. Transfer to a warmed serving bowl, and then sprinkle with the remaining ½ tablespoon thyme. Serve right away.

½ lb (250 g) carrots

½ lb (250 g) parsnips

½ lb (250 g) small white turnips

½ lb (250 g) celery root

½ lb (250 g) small red potatoes

1 whole head of garlic, separated into cloves

¼ cup (2 fl oz/60 ml) extra-virgin olive oil

2 tablespoons chopped fresh thyme

Kosher salt and freshly ground pepper

SERVES 6

Try this dish when you're serving a crowd at an autumn get-together. Halved acorn squashes make perfect individual portions. Halfway through roasting, the halves are filled with maple syrup, balsamic vinegar, lemon juice, and a butter mixture that becomes a sweet-and-sour sauce that pools in the cavity.

MAPLE-BALSAMIC ACORN SQUASH

4 acorn squash, about 6 lb (3 kg) total weight, halved lengthwise and seeded

½ cup (4 fl oz/125 ml) maple syrup

¼ cup (2 fl oz/60 ml) balsamic vinegar

2 tablespoons fresh lemon juice

8 teaspoons unsalted butter

Freshly grated nutmeg

SERVES 8

Preheat the oven to 375°F (190°C).

Cut each squash in half lengthwise and, using a large spoon, scoop out and discard the seeds and strings. Place the squash halves cut side up in a large baking dish. In a small bowl, stir together the maple syrup, vinegar, and lemon juice. Using a pastry brush, brush about half the mixture over the top of the squash.

Roast for about 20 minutes, then brush the squash again with the maple syrup mixture. Divide any remaining mixture among the cavities and add 1 teaspoon butter to each. Sprinkle nutmeg lightly over the squash.

Return to the oven and roast until the squash is tender when pierced with a knife, another 20 minutes. Serve right away, directly out of the baking dish.

In a moderately hot oven, brussels sprouts caramelize around the edges and take on an intensified earthy flavor. Toasted hazelnuts add crunch, while a drizzle of hazelnut oil just before serving adds smooth, round richness.

BRUSSELS SPROUTS WITH TOASTED HAZELNUTS

½ cup (2 oz/60 g) hazelnuts

1½ lb (750 g) brussels sprouts

5 tablespoons (2½ fl oz/ 75 ml) olive oil

Kosher salt and freshly ground pepper

1½ tablespoons Champagne vinegar or white wine vinegar

1 tablespoon hazelnut oil

SERVES 4–6

Preheat the oven to 400°F (200°C).

In a small frying pan over medium-low heat, toast the hazelnuts until they turn deep brown and the nuts smell fragrant, 5 minutes. While the nuts are still warm, wrap them in a clean kitchen towel. Rub the nuts vigorously to remove the skins (it is fine if some bits of skin remain). Coarsely chop the hazelnuts and set aside.

Trim the stem ends of the brussels sprouts and cut each sprout in half lengthwise. Transfer to a large bowl. Drizzle with 3 tablespoons of the olive oil and sprinkle generously with salt and pepper; toss to coat. Transfer to a baking sheet and spread them out in a single layer.

Roast the brussels sprouts, stirring 1 or 2 times, until they are browned in spots and just tender when pierced with a knife, 30–35 minutes.

Remove the baking sheet from the oven and transfer the brussels sprouts to a warmed serving bowl. Toss with the vinegar, the remaining 2 tablespoons olive oil, and the hazelnut oil. Add the toasted hazelnuts, and toss again. Season to taste with salt. Serve right away.

With its unique tan-and-green striped exterior, delicata squash makes a beautiful dinnertime presentation. Its sweet, golden flesh turns even sweeter in a hot oven, and its skin is edible, which makes for an easy preparation.

Preheat the oven to 400°F (200°C).

In a small bowl, stir together the oil and sage, and let steep while you prepare the squash.

Cut the squash in half lengthwise and, using a large spoon, scoop out and discard the seeds and strings. Cut each half into 4 equal pieces. Place the squash on a rimmed baking sheet and drizzle with the sage oil. Using your fingers, distribute the oil to coat the squash all over. Sprinkle with salt and pepper.

Roast the squash until it is browned in spots and tender when pierced with a fork, 45–55 minutes. Transfer to a warmed platter and garnish with the sage sprigs. Serve right away.

ROASTED DELICATA SQUASH WITH SAGE

¼ cup (2 fl oz/60 ml) extra-virgin olive oil

2 tablespoons finely chopped fresh sage, plus 1 or 2 sprigs for garnish

1 delicata squash, about 1½ lb (680 g)

Kosher salt and freshly ground pepper

SERVES 4

Fragrant curry powder heightens the natural sweetness of parsnips to produce a side dish ideal for serving alongside roasted pork or chicken. Fresh lime juice squeezed over the parsnips just before serving makes all the flavors pop.

CURRY-LIME PARSNIPS

Preheat the oven to 400°F (200°C).

Put the butter in a roasting pan just large enough to hold the parsnips in a single layer, and place in the oven as it preheats. Watch carefully to prevent burning. When the butter has melted, remove the pan from the oven, add the sliced parsnips, and toss to coat. Sprinkle evenly with the curry powder and salt and pepper. Stir again, and then arrange the parsnips in a single layer.

Roast the parsnips, stirring 2 or 3 times, until deeply browned and tender when pierced with a fork, 30–40 minutes.

Remove the pan from the oven and transfer the parsnips to a warmed serving bowl. Serve right away, passing the lime wedges at the table for each diner to squeeze over their portion.

2 tablespoons unsalted butter

1 lb (500 g) parsnips, peeled and quartered lengthwise

1 teaspoon Madras curry powder

Kosher salt and freshly ground pepper

4 lime wedges

SERVES 4

In the fall, look for small squash for this recipe, as they cook more evenly than large vegetables. Plus, half a squash is the perfect size for an individual serving. The butter and herb mixture in the squash cavities turns brown in the oven, developing a nutty taste.

BROWN BUTTER WINTER SQUASH

2 small winter squash, such as butternut or acorn, about 1 lb (500 g) each

2 tablespoons extra-virgin olive oil

Kosher salt and freshly ground pepper

2 tablespoons unsalted butter

1 tablespoon chopped fresh herbs, such as sage, thyme, rosemary, or marjoram

SERVES 4

Preheat the oven to 400°F (200°C).

Lightly oil a rimmed baking sheet. Cut each squash in half lengthwise and, using a large spoon, scoop out and discard the seeds and strings. Brush the squash all over with the oil. Season the cut sides generously with salt and pepper, then place the halves cut side down on the prepared baking sheet.

Roast the squash until tender when pierced with a knife, about 20 minutes. Remove the pan from the oven and, using a spatula, carefully turn each half cut side up. Divide the butter into 4 equal pieces and place a piece in each squash cavity. Sprinkle each cavity with the herb of choice, dividing it evenly. Continue to roast until the butter is melted and begins to darken, 5–10 minutes.

Remove the pan from the oven. Using a spatula, transfer the squash to warmed individual plates. Serve right away.

In this straightforward, yet flavorful recipe, mild cauliflower is a great foil for savory olives and tangy lemon zest. It's a perfect dish for cold-weather weeknight meals, as it calls for just four primary ingredients and cooks to tenderness in just 15 minutes.

ROASTED CAULIFLOWER WITH LEMON & OLIVES

Preheat the oven to 400°F (200°C).

Trim the cauliflower and cut it into 2-inch (5-cm) florets. In a shallow roasting pan large enough to hold the cauliflower in a single layer, combine the cauliflower florets, oil, olives, and lemon zest. Sprinkle with salt and pepper and toss to coat. Arrange the ingredients in a single layer.

Roast the cauliflower, stirring occasionally, until browned and tender when pierced with a fork, about 15 minutes. Transfer to a warmed serving dish and serve right away.

1 head cauliflower, about 1½ lb (750 g)

⅓ cup (3 fl oz/80 ml) olive oil

½ cup (75 g) pitted green olives, such as Cerignola, roughly chopped

Zest of 1 lemon

Kosher salt and freshly ground pepper

SERVES 6

This simple dish takes advantage of the whole head of broccoli—even the usually discarded stems. You can also make this dish with broccolini, broccoli's smaller, sweeter, more tender cousin.

SPICY ROASTED BROCCOLI WITH GARLIC

1½ lb (750 g) broccoli heads, trimmed

¼ cup (2 fl oz/60 ml) extra-virgin olive oil

3 tablespoons fresh lemon juice, plus more for serving

3 cloves garlic, minced

Pinch of red pepper flakes

Sea salt

SERVES 4–6

Preheat the oven to 400°F (200°C).

Cut the broccoli lengthwise into spears 4–6 inches (10–15 cm) long. Using a vegetable peeler or a sharp paring knife, remove any dried or bruised skin from the stems. Arrange the spears in a single layer in a roasting pan. Drizzle with the oil, then sprinkle with the lemon juice, garlic, and red pepper flakes. Toss to coat.

Roast, turning once about halfway through cooking time, until the broccoli is tender and the tips and outer edges are crisp and browned, about 15 minutes. Serve right away with an extra squeeze of lemon juice and sea salt, to taste.

Shallots are a delicious alternative to the classic pearl onions for a holiday meal. Here, they are flavored with sage and reduced sherry, which complements the sweet onion flavor.

Preheat the oven to 400°F (200°C).

In a 10-inch (25-cm) pie dish or baking dish, combine the shallots and oil with 1 teaspoon dried sage, ½ teaspoon salt, and a grinding of pepper. Toss to coat. Roast, stirring once or twice, until the shallots are golden and tender, about 45 minutes.

Meanwhile, pour the sherry into a small frying pan and bring to a boil over medium-high heat. Boil gently until reduced by half, about 5 minutes.

Remove the dish from the oven, sprinkle the shallots with the remaining 1 teaspoon dried sage, and pour the reduced sherry on top. Season to taste with salt and pepper and toss to coat. Transfer to a warmed serving dish and serve right away.

PAN-ROASTED SHALLOTS WITH SHERRY

2 lb (1 kg) shallots, peeled, halved lengthwise if large

2 tablespoons olive oil

2 teaspoons dried sage

Kosher salt and freshly ground pepper

¾ cup (6 fl oz/180 ml) sweet sherry

SERVES 4–6

Roasting bananas enhances their sweetness and softens their texture. While the bananas are roasting, the heavy cream and the banana juices meld into a thick sauce. Be sure to choose bananas that are just ripe; overripe bananas will turn mushy.

CINNAMON-ROASTED BANANA SUNDAE

6 large firm-yet-ripe bananas, peeled

¼ teaspoon ground cinnamon

¼ teaspoon ground nutmeg

1–2 tablespoons granulated sugar

2 tablespoons heavy cream

FOR THE CHOCOLATE SAUCE

12 oz (375 g) semisweet chocolate, chopped

2 oz (60 g) unsweetened chocolate, chopped

1½ cups (12 fl oz/375 ml) heavy cream

1 tablespoon vanilla extract, plus additional as needed

1½ qt (1.5 l) cinnamon or vanilla ice cream

SERVES 6

Preheat the oven to 375°F (190°C).

Arrange the bananas in a single layer in a small baking pan. Lightly dust them with the cinnamon, nutmeg, and granulated sugar. Drizzle with the heavy cream.

Roast until the bananas have softened but still hold their shape and the reduced cream forms a bubbly sauce, about 30 minutes.

Meanwhile, make the chocolate sauce: In a large heatproof bowl set over (but not touching) simmering water in a saucepan, melt the chocolates together. Pour in the cream in a steady stream, whisking constantly until well incorporated. The chocolate may "seize," and become lumpy for a moment or two, but just continue to whisk until the sauce becomes smooth. Stir in the vanilla; taste and adjust the flavoring. Keep warm.

When the bananas are ready, arrange them on warmed individual plates, and drizzle the sauce from the pan over the top. Top each with a scoop of ice cream and drizzle with some warm chocolate sauce. Serve right away, passing the remaining hot chocolate sauce at the table.

ROASTED STONE FRUITS WITH VANILLA-SCENTED RICOTTA

1 cup (8 oz/250 g) fresh
whole-milk ricotta

¼ cup (2 oz/60 g)
crème fraîche

½ teaspoon vanilla extract

6 tablespoons (3 oz/90 g)
sugar

2 peaches

2 nectarines

3 plums

8 fresh figs

1 tablespoon melted butter

Honey, for serving

SERVES 6–8

A spoonful of these roasted fruits is like eating a cobbler without the crust. Ricotta drizzled with honey lends a lush creaminess.

Preheat the oven to 475°F (245°C).

In a bowl, stir together the ricotta, crème fraîche, vanilla, and 2 tablespoons of the sugar. Cover and refrigerate until ready to use.

Halve the peaches, nectarines, and plums, and remove the pits. Cut the halves in half again, if desired. Trim off the hard tip of each fig stem and leave the figs whole. Arrange all the fruits in a roasting pan large enough to fit them in a single layer. Drizzle them with the melted butter, and sprinkle with the remaining 4 tablespoons (2 oz/60 g) sugar. Turn to coat.

Roast until the fruits are slightly collapsed and golden or lightly charred, 15–20 minutes.

To serve, spoon the fruits and their cooking juices into warmed individual bowls. Put the ricotta mixture in a serving bowl and drizzle with honey. Serve right away, passing the ricotta mixture at the table.

Good fresh figs are hard to come by. When you see them at the market in the spring and fall, snap them up for this inventive dessert.

━━━━━━━━━━━━━━━━━━━━━━━━━━━━

Preheat the oven to 425°F (220°C).

In a small saucepan, combine the honey, butter, vinegar, peppercorns, and a tiny pinch of salt. Heat over medium-low until the butter has melted and the mixture loosens into a sauce, about 5 minutes.

Lightly oil a 10-inch (25-cm) cast-iron frying pan or baking dish. Using a small, sharp knife and starting at the blossom ends, cut each fig into quarters, stopping just short of cutting through the stem ends so the quarters are still attached. Carefully arrange the figs standing upright in the prepared pan and nudge the cut ends open like flower petals. Spoon the sauce over the figs.

Roast until the figs are softened and lightly caramelized, 10–15 minutes. Using a large spoon, carefully transfer the figs to a warmed serving platter and garnish with the mint sprigs. Place a dollop of mascarpone or vanilla ice cream next to the figs, if desired, and drizzle with the sauce from the baking dish. Serve right away.

ROASTED FIGS WITH BALSAMIC, HONEY & BLACK PEPPER

2 tablespoons wildflower or other full-flavored honey

1 tablespoon unsalted butter

1 tablespoon aged balsamic vinegar

½ teaspoon peppercorns, lightly crushed

Sea salt

Vegetable oil, for greasing

12 ripe fresh Mission or Calimyrna figs

Small fresh mint sprigs, for garnish

Mascarpone or vanilla ice cream for serving (optional)

SERVES 4–6

Roasted spiced apples are appealing on their own, but topped with crisp, buttered bread crumbs, they are positively irresistible. To make the bread crumbs, choose a simple coarse bread with a firm texture, such as a rustic Italian or French bread. Let the bread sit out overnight, or dry the slices in a low oven, then remove the crust. Chop the bread coarsely, and use a food processor to reduce the pieces to coarse crumbs.

ROASTED APPLES WITH SPICED BREAD CRUMBS

Place an oven rack in the lower third of the oven and preheat to 375°F (190°C). Lightly grease a 9-inch (23-cm) baking pan.

Spread the bread crumbs on a rimmed baking sheet and toast in the oven until lightly golden, about 10 minutes. Let cool.

In a large bowl, stir together the granulated sugar, brown sugar, cinnamon, nutmeg, and toasted bread crumbs. Add the apple slices and toss to coat. Place a third of the apple mixture in the prepared baking dish and dot with a third of the butter. Repeat twice, finishing with the butter.

Roast until the apples are tender when pierced with a knife and the bread crumbs are golden brown, 1–1¼ hours. Serve right away with a drizzle of cream, if desired.

½ cup (4 oz/125 g) unsalted butter, cut into small pieces and brought to room temperature, plus extra for greasing

3 cups (6 oz/185 g) coarse fresh bread crumbs

½ cup (4 oz/125 g) granulated sugar

½ cup (3½ oz/105 g) firmly packed golden brown sugar

½ teaspoon ground cinnamon

½ teaspoon freshly grated nutmeg

4 firm, tart apples, peeled, halved, cored, and very thinly sliced (about 6 cups/1½ lb/750 g)

Heavy cream at room temperature, for serving (optional)

SERVES 6–8

ROASTED PLUMS WITH GINGER-OAT TOPPING

2 lb (1 kg) ripe dark purple plums, pitted and quartered

½ cup (2 ox/60 g) crystallized ginger pieces, finely chopped

½ cup (1 1/2 oz/45 g) old-fashioned rolled oats

½ cup (4 oz/125 g) sugar

6 tablespoons (3 oz/90 g) unsalted butter, at room temperature

¼ cup (1½ oz/45 g) all-purpose flour

Vanilla ice cream for serving

SERVES 6–8

Plums proliferate in the summer and into fall. This recipe, like a miniature fruit crisp, is a great way to use them when they fill the stalls at the farmers' market. Use the same technique for other stone fruits like peaches, nectarines, and pluots.

Preheat the oven to 400°F (200°C).

Put the plums in a buttered shallow 8-inch (20-cm) baking pan just large enough to hold them comfortably. Toss the plums with the candied ginger. Set aside.

In a food processor, combine the oats, sugar, butter, and flour. Pulse for a few seconds until the ingredients are coarsely chopped. The mixture will clump together. Sprinkle the oat mixture evenly over the plums.

Roast until the plums are bubbling and the top is browned, about 30 minutes.

Scoop the ice cream into dessert bowls and spoon the warm plums on the top.

This is a great dish to serve on a rainy summertime evening, when nectarines are at their prime but it's too wet outside to grill. The Caribbean-inspired toppings of raw sugar and dark rum evoke tropical weather indoors.

NECTARINES WITH RAW SUGAR & RUM

1 tablespoon butter

4 nectarines, halved and pitted

3 tablespoons turbinado sugar

3 tablespoons dark rum

SERVES 4

Preheat the oven to 375°F (190°C).

Spread the butter evenly in a baking dish just large enough to hold nectarine halves in a single layer. Arrange the nectarines cut side up in the prepared dish. In a small bowl, stir together the sugar and rum. Divide the mixture among the nectarine cavities.

Roast until the sugar has melted and the nectarines have softened but still hold their shape, 10–15 minutes. Serve warm.

Here is an innovative dessert sure to be a conversation starter: Fresh pineapple slices are flavored with brown sugar, vanilla extract, and black pepper, then roasted to a scorched finish. Lightly sweetened yogurt is spooned over the top, adding richness to temper the bold flavors.

ROASTED PINEAPPLE WITH BLACK PEPPER & VANILLA

1 large ripe pineapple

½ cup (4 oz/125 g) firmly packed golden brown sugar

½ teaspoon vanilla extract

Freshly ground pepper

½ cup (4 oz/125 g) plain Greek yogurt

Confectioners' sugar (optional)

SERVES 4

Preheat the oven to 425°F (220°C).

Place the pineapple upright on a cutting board and twist or cut off the leaves. Using a long slicing knife, cut off the top and bottom inch of the pineapple. Place your knife on top of the fruit and slice down to the bottom of the pineapple, removing the skin and rotating as needed. Once you've removed the skin, slice off any remaining brown spots or "eyes" on the surface of the flesh. Cut the pineapple in half lengthwise. Cut away the core and place each half, flat side down, on the cutting board. Cut crosswise into slices ½ inch (12 mm) thick.

Arrange the pineapple slices, slightly overlapping, in a shallow baking dish.

In a small bowl, stir together the brown sugar, ¼ teaspoon of the vanilla extract, and ¼–½ teaspoon pepper. Sprinkle the mixture evenly over the pineapple. Roast until the pineapple is glazed on top and tender when pierced with a fork, 20–25 minutes, depending on the ripeness of the pineapple. Let cool.

Whisk the remaining ¼ teaspoon vanilla extract into the yogurt. Stir in confectioners' sugar, if using, to your desired sweetness.

To serve, arrange 2 or 3 slices pineapple on individual plates. Spoon some of the cooking juices over the slices, and top with a dollop of the yogurt. Serve right away.

INDEX